D1571167

Shakespeare's Last Plays:
A New Approach

Shakespeare's Last Plays: A New Approach

Frances A. Yates

LONDON

Routledge & Kegan Paul

First published in 1975
by Routledge & Kegan Paul Ltd
Broadway House, 68–74 Carter Lane
London EC4V 5EL
Set in Monotype Perpetua
and printed in Great Britain
by Ebenezer Baylis and Son Limited
The Trinity Press, Worcester, and London

Contents

Contents

Plates

Plates

Preface

The title of this book is the same as that of the series of four Lord
Northcliffe Lectures in Literature which I delivered in January
1974, at University College, London, by kind invitation of the
Provost, Lord Annan, and of the then Lord Northcliffe Professor
of Modern English Literature at University College, Frank Kermode. The subject of the lectures was left to me, and I chose to
take the opportunity, so generously afforded to me, of thinking
over in the presence of a very friendly and encouraging audience,
certain ideas concerning Shakespeare's relation to the problems
and thought currents of his times.

The first four chapters of this book represent the lectures,
almost exactly as given, save for necessary transitions in style
from the spoken to the written word and a few minor revisions.
The illustrations are the same as those used in the slides shown
with the first lecture. The four lecture-chapters are preceded by
an Introduction which outlines some of my earlier work. It was
felt that readers of this book who do not know my other books
would need such a guide, since this study grows out of my earlier
labours. My own feeling also was that it might palliate the
audacity of trying to say something 'new' about Shakespeare in
such a small volume, if it were indicated in an Introduction that
the present book has more than forty years of research into the
cultural history of the Renaissance behind it. The last part of

the Introduction, on the present state of Shakespearean scholarship about the Last Plays, originally formed the opening of the first Northcliffe Lecture.

The fifth chapter, on Ben Jonson and the Last Plays, is quite new and formed no part of the lectures. I had formulated the Ben Jonson material before giving the lectures but decided not to attempt to introduce it into them. I have added it here because Ben Jonson's adverse attitude to the themes of the Last Plays helps greatly towards our understanding of them and of Shakespeare.

In a brief Epilogue I have touched on some of the ways in which the theme of this book might relate to the history of thought. The questions raised are indeed large, and such an Epilogue had to be either very long or very short. I chose to make it very short, only a whisper, as it were, as to what might come out of this line of approach to Shakespeare.

I want to emphasise that word 'approach' in my title. This book is an approach only, not a final arrival at a destination. And it is an approach only to Shakespeare's Last Plays, though it is impossible to divide these off from Shakespeare as a whole. One way of putting this attempt might be to say that the elucidation of the historical situation behind the Last Plays provides a new point of entry into Shakespearean problems as a whole.

I have kept the annotation light because I want this book to go out quickly so that others can begin to think about, and criticise, its argument. This argument concerns Shakespearean scholars; it concerns historians; and it concerns historians of thought, particularly those interested in the Hermetic aspects of Renaissance culture. Above all it is addressed quite simply to all those who are fascinated by Shakespeare, from whatever point of view. The possibility has arisen that the serious historical and critical approach to subjects formerly dismissed as 'occult', and left to the mercy of pseudo-scholarship, might now bring us close to a new understanding of Shakespeare, and mitigate the sensationalism and conjecture which have surrounded this extraordinary figure. My last plea to the reader of this book is that he should read it critically and carefully, if possible dismissing from his mind all the old myths in order to be free to make quite a new 'approach'.

Acknowledgments

Permission for the quotation of passages from the introduction by R. A. Foakes to the Arden edition of Shakespeare's *Henry VIII* was given by the publishers, Methuen and Co., Ltd.

The 'Rainbow Portrait' is reproduced by courtesy of the Marquis of Salisbury. I have also to thank the following for permission to reproduce photographs: the Fitzwilliam Museum, Cambridge; the President and Fellows of Magdalen College, Oxford and the Royal Academy of Arts; the Trustees of the Chatsworth Settlement and the Courtauld Institute of Art; the Trustees of the British Museum.

Warburg Institute

Introduction

Looking back, it seems to me that I have always had behind me, or within, the thought of Shakespeare, of when and where my studies drew near to him, or withdrew far from him. Many years ago, moving along the Strand with Giordano Bruno as I endeavoured to translate his *Cena de le ceneri* and began to realise what his great *impresa* was – the dissemination of a magical philosophy which should do away with all religious differences on a level of love and magic – Shakespeare seemed to come to join that journey to the Supper Party. Later, Bruno's Hermetic version of the art of memory seemed to raise the question whether here might be a clue to the vast powers of Shakespeare's imagination. But the time for writing a book on 'Shakespeare and the Hermetic Tradition' had not come, nor has it yet come, though this book might be an 'approach' to it.

All my studies seem to have been linked together; each effort has led on inevitably to the next. I suppose that the sequence began when I first entered the French embassy in London in the time of Elizabeth I and met there *John Florio: An Italian in Shakespeare's England*[1] and Florio's friend, Giordano Bruno. Already the problem arose of what was the nature of Bruno's mission in England and why he was staying at the French embassy. Florio led to Shakespeare and to a premature attempt at solving so-called topical allusions in *Love's Labour's Lost*.[2] The French

3

academy mentioned in that play, attended by courtiers belonging to opposite sides in the French wars of religion, seemed to call for more explanation than had hitherto been available. The resultant book, *The French Academies of the Sixteenth Century*,[3] led into the encyclopedia of knowledge as understood in the Renaissance Neoplatonic tradition. These French Academies turned out to be concerned with supplying the techniques for expressing in dramatic and musical form in the contemporary French court festivals this complex and profound outlook. They were also concerned in bringing together poets and musicians of opposite religious parties to co-operate in the production of music with good 'effects' as part of the effort of toleration and conciliation attempted through the festivals encouraged by Catherine de' Medici. It began to seem that the French academy in *Love's Labour's Lost*, with the names of its members taken from opposite sides in the French wars of religion, its production of a mysterious masque and dance, its conclusion in an atmosphere of mutual good will and charity, might be a more significant type of topical allusion in the play than the little point of whether or not Florio was the original of Holofernes.

John Florio performed the most valuable service of attracting the attention of the scholars of the Warburg Institute, then but newly arrived in England. I was made free of vast new stores of knowledge in a library designed for the assistance of the Renaissance scholar, and was initiated into the Warburgian technique of using visual evidence as historical evidence. A long-standing interest in the symbolic presentation of Queen Elizabeth I, in pageantry, poetry, and portraits, took shape in the study of 'Queen Elizabethan I as Astraea', first published in article form at that time, and republished in 1974 in *Astraea*.[4]

The dominant theme of the Elizabethan age, so *Astraea* argues, was the idea of imperial reform. The Tudor reform of the Church, carried out by the Monarch, allowed the propagandists of that reform to draw upon the traditions and symbolism of sacred empire for the glorification of the Queen. The image of her as Astraea, the Just Virgin of the Imperial Reform, was built up during her reign in the complex symbolism used of her, which incorporated the legend of the Trojan descent of the Tudors with the religious imperialism. This propaganda accustomed the public to think of a purified Church and Empire as a woman. The 'Sieve' portrait of the Queen as a Vestal Virgin has exactly the same notional content as Shakespeare's line on a 'Vestal thronèd by the West'.

The cult of the Imperial Virgin found its most congenial expression in the pageantry of chivalry. The Accession Day Tilts, held during the reign of Elizabeth I on the anniversaries of her accession, were occasions for the deployment of the Elizabeth symbolism. That the contemporary pageants of chivalry were the inspiration of Spenser's *Faerie Queene*, the epic expressive of the Elizabethan imperial idea, is argued in the essay on Elizabethan Chivalry, reprinted in *Astraea*.[5] The Queen was presented as a Triumph of Chastity[6] in this chivalric symbolism, an idea connected with that of the purity of her reformed religion, which entered deeply into Elizabethan Protestantism, in which there was an element of Puritanism expressed through courtly and chivalric forms.

The arguments and studies in *Astraea* prepare the ground for the present book in which the same type of iconographical study is continued into the early Jacobean period. In this period there was an Elizabethan revival, centred on James I's children, Henry and Elizabeth, and the Elizabethan symbolism and ideology was used in connection with them. This is the theme of the first chapter of this book and in later chapters it is argued that Shakespeare's Last Plays reflect in their imagery this Elizabethan revival within the Jacobean age. The methods of *Astraea* are thus here applied to Shakespeare interpretation.

It is important to compare the propaganda for the monarchy in the Elizabethan age with that surrounding the idea of the French monarchy in contemporary France.[7] Here, war between Protestants and Catholics nearly destroyed the monarchy, a situation which might also have arisen in England. In France, too, the destiny of monarchy was in the hands of a woman, Catherine de'

Medici. The methods which she tried for holding together the dangerous situation were only partially successful. The great court festivals which she organised were a revival of Franco-Burgundian chivalry in all its trappings, with Renaissance influences added. In them, the opposite religious parties were invited to join together in common loyalty to the monarchy. The ethos of the series of 'politique' French festivals is studied in *The Valois Tapestries*,[8] an illustrated study of those tapestries which reflect the festivals at the Valois court. These festivals influenced the English chivalric movement. 'Prince Henry's Barriers', studied in this book, belongs to the type of courtly exercise which is illustrated, in its French form, in the tapestries.

The last of the Valois festivals, the 'Magnificences' of 1581 for the wedding of the Duc de Joyeuse, receive more detailed attention in articles reprinted in *Astraea* which show the close connection between these festivals, which are the last fruit of the cult of incantatory Poetry and Music in the French Academy,[9] and Henri III's 'politique' religious movement,[10] menaced and destroyed by the Catholic League, but which led on to the religious settlement under Henri IV.[11] Giordano Bruno's mission to England belongs to the atmosphere of France under Henri III, and these studies suggest further the influence of these movements on Shakespeare's idea of a French academy in *Love's Labour's Lost*.

Such iconographical studies, continued in this book in relation to Shakespeare's Last Plays, constitute one branch of the 'new approach'. The other line of approach is through the study of Hermetic influences in these plays, which has also been prepared through a good deal of earlier work.

In *Giordano Bruno and the Hermetic Tradition*,[12] Bruno was presented as a Renaissance magus, deriving from the Renaissance revival of magic, from the traditions of Magia and Cabala ultimately stemming from the work of Marsilio Ficino and Pico della Mirandola and standardised in Cornelius Agrippa's textbook of 'occult philosophy'. Though there is so much that is original in Bruno's Italian dialogues, published in England from 1582 to

1585, it was demonstrated that he makes long quotations from Hermetic sources and undeniably belongs to a rather extremely magical form of the Hermetic tradition. He preaches in these dialogues, not only his new philosophy of heliocentricity, but also a programme of moral reform shown forth in the images of the constellations (an idea possibly suggested to him by the great model of the heavens at the Joyeuse festivals), and a revived magical religion through which religious controversy would be dissolved in higher insights. The familiar journey along the Strand had to be taken again in this book with these new revelations in mind. Nor was Bruno marginal for the Elizabethan Renaissance, if, as rumoured, Philip Sidney knew him. These questions were further explored in *The Art of Memory*[13] in which Bruno's Hermetic versions of the art were found to contain the core of his message and to have attracted very great interest in Elizabethan London.

Whilst the visit of Bruno brought a strong new infusion of Hermetic influences into Shakespeare's England, associating these with the politico-religious situation in an outlook antagonistic to the Spanish-Hapsburg ambitions in Europe, a native Hermetic magus had long been highly influential in the Elizabethan age. This was John Dee, a magus formed on Agrippa's 'occult philosophy' and who associated Hermetic tradition with a strong development of mathematics. Dee is the centre of *Theatre of the World*[14] in which the influence of Vitruvius on his mathematical preface to Euclid is studied, and it is indicated that Robert Fludd, thh 'Rosicrucian', comes out of the Dee tradition, and, probably, also Inigo Jones. Dee permeated the whole Elizabethan age, from the Queen downwards. That he was the inspiration of Shakespeare's Prospero is very strongly indicated in the present book by comparing *The Tempest* with Ben Jonson's attack on Dee in *The Alchemist*, which can be confirmed from the study of Dee in *Theatre of the World*.

My last study of Hermetic traditions stemming from the Renaissance was *The Rosicrucian Enlightenment*.[15] This book starts from the same historical moment as does *Shakespeare's Last Plays*.

It begins with the marriage of Princess Elizabeth and the Elector Palatine in 1613 and suggests that the German Rosicrucian movement was, in part, aroused by influences from England stimulated by the English alliance. The philosophy behind the German Rosicrucian manifestos was the philosophy of John Dee, and the myth of 'Christian Rosencreutz' in which it is expressed may owe something to the Red Cross Knight, that is to say to esoteric influences embodied in English chivalric tradition. Rosicrucianism is seen as a last phase in the Renaissance Hermetic-Cabalist tradition, in which Paracelsist alchemy joins with other influences to form a mystical religious movement which attracted liberal thinkers in the years before the Thirty Years' War. The romance by Johann Valentin Andreae, *The Chemical Wedding of Christian Rosencreutz*, is believed to reflect the court of the Princess Elizabeth and the Elector Palatine at Heidelberg, and to express in mythical language the Rosicrucian aspirations around them. The movement used theatrical forms of expression, influenced by the travelling companies of English players in Germany.

The present book connects very closely with *The Rosicrucian Enlightenment*, for influences similar to those in that movement are discovered in Shakespeare's Last Plays.

Thus all my former 'approaches' to the Renaissance lie behind the approach to Shakespeare in this book. The analysis of imagery of the type studied in *Astraea* to elucidate the Elizabethan age is carried further here to elucidate the Elizabethan revival around Prince Henry and Princess Elizabeth in the Jacobean age. This imagery is found reflected in Shakespeare's Last Plays, thus associating them with a historical moment. The Rosicrucian ideas studied in *The Rosicrucian Enlightenment* are disengaged from the Last Plays, showing that Shakespeare's thought in these plays belongs to the evolution of the Renaissance Hermetic-Cabalist tradition into Rosicrucianism.

It is thus claimed that the new approach to the Last Plays in this book, arising out of many years of previous effort, enables one to place Shakespeare in a historical context, both as to actual historical events and as to the thought-movements accompanying them. This approach certainly does not explain Shakespeare nor the Last Plays, many episodes and problems in which are left quite unexplored here. It aims at providing the suggestion of new routes, hitherto more or less unsuspected, into Shakespearean problems through which these problems might eventually be given a new historical dimension.

A guiding theme through all these researches has been interest in the history of religion. Behind Bruno, the philosopher, was sought Bruno, the *illuminatus*, propagating an esoteric religion. Within the imagery used of the Virgin Queen was sought the meaning which chastity had for Elizabethan chivalry and its esoteric Puritanism. French festivals revealed that a series of French court festivals might be ultimately inspired by an aim of bringing together warring religious factions in an atmosphere of Neoplatonism diffused in French Academies. And so we are led to look in the Last Plays for meanings which might reveal to us the nature of Shakespeare's religion in his last years and through what historical channels he looked to see his religious hopes fulfilled.

Concerning the facts about Shakespeare's Last Plays, concerning texts, dates, sources, and so on, I rely mainly on the New Arden edition of the plays in which the latest scholarship is so admirably presented, though I have also used other critical studies. My reading of these has brought home to me with renewed force, the accuracy and skill, the patient and careful work, of the best Shakespearean textual and literary scholarship, to which I have contributed nothing. It is upon the work of others that I attempt to raise the structure of these new approaches and before beginning to do so I must try to resume, briefly and inexpertly, what is the state of expert Shakespearean scholarship about the Last Plays.

The earliest of them may be *Pericles*,[16] which cannot be later than 1608 and could be earlier. It was printed in 1609 and reprinted several times in the following years. Unlike all the other Last Plays it was not included by Heminges and Condell in their First Folio edition of Shakespeare's plays published in 1623.

This caused doubt to be cast on *Pericles* as possibly not by Shakespeare. Yet much of it sounds truly Shakespearean and in its themes and atmosphere it is very close to the group of the Last Plays. It is now accepted as Shakespearean, though some scenes are by a collaborator.

Performances of *The Winter's Tale*[17] and of *Cymbeline*[18] were seen by Simon Forman in 1611 who noted down a brief description of their plots which corresponds to the plots of these plays as we have them, though with some items and names omitted. Forman states that he saw *The Winter's Tale* at the Globe and it was probably also at the Globe that he saw *Cymbeline*, though he does not state this. *The Winter's Tale* was acted again in the Christmas season of 1612 when it was one of the plays by Shakespeare given before the Princess Elizabeth and the Elector Palatine as part of the festivities for their wedding.[19] *Cymbeline* is not mentioned in the list of plays given before the Princess and her betrothed, although this play is closely related to *The Winter's Tale* and shares with that play the similar experiences of having been seen by Forman in 1611 and first printed in the Folio of 1623.

The most famous of the Last Plays is, of course, *The Tempest*.[20] Apparently Simon Forman did not see it in 1611 when he saw *The Winter's Tale* and *Cymbeline*, since he does not mention it. *The Tempest* was, however, in existence in 1611 since a play of that name was performed at court in that year. It was one of the plays performed before the Princess Elizabeth and the Elector Palatine in 1612. It was first printed in the First Folio of 1623 where it is the first play in the volume.

Henry VIII[21] was also first printed in the First Folio of 1623. In spite of this acceptance by Heminges and Condell, doubt used to be cast on Shakespeare's authorship of the play. These doubts are now largely dispersed and it is treated as mostly, if not all, by Shakespeare. One of the reasons for this acceptance is the fact that modern scholarship about the Last Plays has brought out that *Henry VIII*, though unlike the other Last Plays in being a straight history play and not a romance, is like them in many of its themes and its mood. It was probably written and performed soon after the marriage of the Princess Elizabeth with the Elector Palatine, and it reflects the pageantry for that wedding. It is the play which was being performed at the Globe when the theatre was burned down in June 1613.

There is one other Last Play, *The Two Noble Kinsmen*,[22] parts of which are now thought to be by Shakespeare, though it is mainly, probably, by John Fletcher. It was first acted at the Blackfriars theatre, probably during the winter of 1613–14, and it reflects the festivals for the wedding of the Princess Elizabeth and the Elector Palatine in a particularly interesting way. Though aspects of this play support my arguments, I have excluded it from discussion here because its textual problems are so complicated.

To resume this history, all the Last Plays except *Pericles* were first printed in the Folio of 1623. *Pericles* is a curious exception, as the only Last Play of which printed editions existed when the Folio editors were collecting the texts, and they excluded it from the Folio, a slight from which that remarkable play has long suffered. For *The Winter's Tale*, *Cymbeline*, *The Tempest* and *Henry VIII* the only available texts are those in the First Folio. We know, however, that *The Winter's Tale*, *Cymbeline*, and *The Tempest* were in existence in 1611 when they were performed. We know that *The Winter's Tale* and *The Tempest* (but not *Cymbeline*) were performed before the Princess Elizabeth and the Elector Palatine in 1612, and that *Henry VIII* was being performed early in 1613.

Shakespeare's Last Plays, therefore, were probably written from about 1608 (if that is the right date for the composition of *Pericles* which is not certain) to early in 1613, that is after the great tragedies but still in the earlier years of the reign of James I.

Much interest has been taken in the Last Plays in recent years from the point of view of staging and stagecraft. They were contemporary with the masques at court designed by Inigo Jones and it is pointed out that the Last Plays have a masque-like quality and may have used scenic effects more elaborate than those which used to be seen at the Globe. Emphasis is laid on the fact that the King's Men, Shakespeare's company, acquired the Blackfriars theatre in 1608 which gave more scope for a new kind of staging. Arguments that the masque-like quality of some of the Last Plays means that Shakespeare designed them for Blackfriars, for a different kind of theatre from the Globe, are weakened by the fact that Simon Forman saw *The Winter's Tale* and probably *Cymbeline*, two of the most masque-like of the plays, at the Globe. The Blackfriars argument should not, therefore, be overdone. Nevertheless in their mood, in their romantic and visionary quality, the Last Plays do undoubtedly impinge on the masque.

Certain themes are common to the Last Plays as a whole, as has been brought out in connection with *Pericles*, *The Winter's Tale*, *Cymbeline* and *The Tempest* in the introductions to those plays in the New Arden edition; also by Wilson Knight in his book *The Crown of Life*,[23] and in other critical studies.[24]

One characteristic is the so-called 'double plot'. Unlike Shakespeare's earlier romantic comedies in which the central figures are lovers, young men and women of marriageable age, the romances of the Last Plays are concerned with families, and with two generations within a family. There are two plots, one concerned with the older people, one with the younger people. The younger generation is usually represented by a daughter and her lover – Marina in *Pericles*, Perdita in *The Winter's Tale*, Miranda in *The Tempest*, Imogen in *Cymbeline*. In *Cymbeline* alone the family of the younger generation is larger, including not only Imogen and her husband but also her two brothers. The action takes a long stretch through time to allow for the growing up of the children. Through the recognition of long-lost children, happy endings are achieved. Old unhappinesses are healed through the action of a younger generation which brings hope for the future. The theme of reconciliation is basic for the Last Plays, the healing of old quarrels and old wounds, the hope of a better future through the younger generation. There is a profound philosophical significance in the plays, a magical sense of interaction between man and nature. The magical atmosphere is also a deeply religious atmosphere, productive of 'theophanies', or new revelations of the divine. The theme of music, typifying restoration of harmony, comes through at points of high emotional significance.

Henry VIII is concerned with real historical characters, with a real king of England and two of his wives, and not with a mythical king, like Cymbeline, or with princes of romance, like Pericles, Leontes, Prospero. Yet the themes characteristic of the Last Plays are present in it – reconciliation, forgiveness, a lapse of time allowing for the appearance of new generations.

Thus the world of the Last Plays, though organically related to Shakespeare's earlier thought, is also a world in itself. Shakespeare was living in the early years of the reign of James I in which many survivors of the Elizabethan age, himself included, were still alive. The King belonged to the older generation, and his early life had been passed at grips with the issues of the late sixteenth century. He had children whom many hailed as the hope of the future, Prince Henry in whom long lost traditions of Protestant activism seemed to be reviving, Princess Elizabeth whose marriage to the Elector Palatine aroused visions of the rebirth of the phoenix, the revival of the old Elizabethan traditions in a new and wider sense.

It is this real situation which was at the back of Shakespeare's mind in the Last Plays, and his deep concern for the issues of his times was behind the poetry which flowed from his genius in these last years.

Notes

1   *John Florio: An Italian in Shakespeare's England*, Cambridge University Press, 1934; Octagon Books, New York, 1968.
2   'A Study of *Love's Labour's Lost*', in *Shakespeare Problems*, ed. A. W. Pollard and J. Dover Wilson, Cambridge University Press, 1936.

3   *The French Academies of the Sixteenth Century*, Warburg Institute, 1947; Kraus Reprint, 1967 (abbreviated hereafter as *Academies*).

4   *Astraea: the Imperial Theme in the Sixteenth Century*, Routledge & Kegan Paul, London and Boston, 1974 (abbreviated hereafter as *Astraea*).

5   'Elizabethan Chivalry: the Romance of the Accession Day Tilts', *Astraea*, pp. 88–111.

6   'The Triumph of Chastity', *Astraea*, pp. 112–20.

7   'The Idea of the French Monarchy', *Astraea*, pp. 121–6.

8   *The Valois Tapestries*, Warburg Institute, 1959; second edn by Routledge & Kegan Paul, London, forthcoming.

9   'The Magnificences for the Marriage of the Duc de Joyeuse, Paris, 1581', *Astraea*, pp. 149–72.

10 'Religious Processions in Paris, 1583–4', *Astraea*, pp. 173–207.

11 'Astraea and the Gallic Hercules', *Astraea*, pp. 208–14.

12 *Giordano Bruno and the Hermetic Tradition*, Routledge & Kegan Paul, London and University of Chicago Press, 1964, reprinted, London, 1971; Vintage Books paperback, New York, 1969 (abbreviated hereafter as *Bruno*).

13 *The Art of Memory*, Routledge & Kegan Paul, London and University of Chicago Press, 1966; Penguin, 1969 (abbreviated hereafter as *Memory*).

14 *Theatre of the World*, Routledge & Kegan Paul, London and University of Chicago Press, 1969 (abbreviated hereafter as *Theatre*).

15 *The Rosicrucian Enlightenment*, Routledge & Kegan Paul, London and Boston, 1972 (abbreviated hereafter as *RE*).

16 *Pericles*, ed. F. D. Hoeniger, Arden edition paperback, 1969.

17 *The Winter's Tale*, ed. J. H. P. Pafford, Arden edition paperback, 1966.

18 *Cymbeline*, ed. J. M. Nosworthy, Arden edition paperback, 1955.

19 The document listing the fourteen plays given on this occasion is printed in E. K. Chambers, *William Shakespeare*, London, 1930, II, p. 343; idem, *The Elizabethan Stage*, London, 1923, II, p. 217.

20 *The Tempest*, ed. F. Kermode, Arden edition paperback, 1964.

21 *Henry VIII*, ed. R. A. Foakes, Arden edition paperback, 1968.

22 J. Fletcher and Shakespeare, *The Two Noble Kinsmen*, ed. G. R. Proudfoot, Regents Renaissance Drama Series, 1970.

23 G. Wilson Knight, *The Crown of Life*, Oxford University Press, 1947; paperback, 1965.

24 Numerous articles are reprinted in *Shakespeare's Later Comedies: an Anthology of Modern Criticism*, ed. D. J. Palmer, Penguin, 1971.

I

The Elizabethan Revival in the Jacobean Age

The consistent and complicated propaganda which had been built around Queen Elizabeth I, had glorified her as the Virgin representative of imperial reform. The Tudor reform of the Church by the Monarch was based on the traditions of sacred imperialism, on the right of emperors in the Councils of the Church. Sacred imperialism was the dominant theme in the propaganda for Elizabeth I, as has been demonstrated in *Astraea*. With this theme of monarchical reformation was associated the chivalrous romance enacted around the Queen by her knights. Through the mythical descent of the Tudors from King Arthur, the Tudor imperial and Protestant reform of the Church could be presented in terms of a pure knighthood obeying the behests of a Virgin Queen and spreading the light of her rule through the world.[1] Thus there was built in to the basically Protestant position of the Queen as representative of a pure reformed Church which had cast off the impurities of Rome, this aura of chivalric Arthurian purity, of a British imperialism, using British in the mythic and romantic sense which it had for the Elizabethans. The Virgil of the Elizabethan religious imperialism immortalised its chivalric modes of expression in *The Faerie Queene*.[2]

James I, when he succeeded to Elizabeth's throne, tried also to succeed to her symbolism. He claimed the descent, through his Tudor ancestor, Henry VII, from King Arthur, and Arthurian associations were used in celebrating the union of Scotland and England brought about through his accession to the two thrones.[3] James as ruler of a united Britain was a new Arthur of Britain. Nevertheless, there were profound differences between the Tudor religious and chivalric imperialism inspired by the Virgin Queen and the more limited conceptions of James. The Elizabethan type implied the establishment of a universal pure reform, a purified order and peace which could appeal to chivalric religious traditions to maintain it. For James, as has been said, 'his British claim became entangled with his concept of divine right which was far more partisan than the broad heavenly blessing ascribed to the Tudors'.[4] The Jacobean peace – and James forever emphasised himself as a peacebringer and peacemaker – was an avoidance of conflict. It carried within it no mission of universal reform or support of European Protestantism.

The uneasiness of James's reign largely arose through this confusion. On the one hand, James appeared to be, both at home and abroad, the successor of Elizabeth, not only to her throne but also to her politics and symbolism, the representative of Protestant monarchy, the leader of Protestant Europe. Yet, though in the beginning of his reign James appeared to be resuming the Elizabethan role of championship of religious reform, of friendship with Protestant princes abroad, at heart he was deeply afraid of the Catholic Spanish-Hapsburg powers, and was bent on appeasing them.

Surviving Elizabethans of the old school, like Philip Sidney's friend, Fulke Greville, or like Walter Raleigh, were acutely aware of the change in temper under James, and anxious about it. And anyone could see the profound difference between the tone of Elizabeth's court, with its emphasis on chastity and dignity, and the court of James. The Elizabethan chivalric Puritanism had suffered an eclipse; the Philip Sidney tradition was in abeyance.

The magical and scientific tradition stemming from John Dee, formerly philosopher-in-chief to Queen Elizabeth, was also in abeyance and discouraged. The discouragement of Dee had begun in the last years of Elizabeth's reign, after his return from his mysterious activities in Bohemia. He appealed to James, after his accession, to defend him from charges of black magic, but in vain.[5] He died in 1608 in great poverty. Dee had been a propagator and theorist of the Elizabethan type of British imperialism; the neglect and discarding of Dee was also, in effect, a denial of a deep-seated Elizabethan movement, with which Philip Sidney had probably been in sympathy.

Yet there was also in this early Jacobean period a movement which might be called an Elizabethan revival, and which was particularly associated with James's eldest son, Prince Henry. From a very early age, this young man had shown signs of remarkable determination of character and capacity for leadership. Prince Henry did not leave a strong mark on history because he was not destined to live to make that mark. He died on 17 November 1612, at the age of nineteen, only two years after becoming Prince of Wales amid general acclamation. We can never know what difference the early and most unexpected death of this young man made in history.

Though the panegyric of Prince Henry by his tutor, Charles Cornwallis,[6] published in 1641, may err on the side of exaggeration, the main lines of his characterisation of the prince are corroborated from other sources, particularly the despatches of the Venetian ambassador, who admired him greatly.[7] Cornwallis describes him as grave beyond his years, reserved and secret. He gathered about him a large household of young men, more than five hundred, whom he led in virtue and discipline and military sports. He was not lascivious, always decorous in behaviour, and singularly graceful in his movements. He was genuinely pious and strongly Protestant, though, according to the Venetian ambassador, he would not allow anyone to call the Pope Antichrist in his presence.[8] The Venetian ambassador hints that Prince Henry entertained schemes of very great weight and scope, that he believed that a way could be found for ending 'the jars in religion'.[9] He also believed in working for strong military and naval preparedness. He and his followers engaged constantly in martial exercises. He was interested in military art, mathematics, and fortification,[10] and particularly interested in shipbuilding. He encouraged Phineas Pett who built for him a ship of war. On military and naval matters he consulted Walter Raleigh, who fared no better than John Dee in the Jacobean age, for James kept him in prison. Everyone knows Prince Henry's remark, that only his father would keep such a bird as that in a cage.

As this remark implies, there was a marked contrast between Prince Henry and his father in character, and in what would now be called public image. The image of Prince Henry, the stern young prince exercising for some coming duty, has about it an aura of Philip Sidney which could never linger over James. Prince Henry's court was more like a continuation of Elizabethan traditions than the court which we think of as Jacobean.

Prince Henry would appear to have been building himself up, and being built up by others, as a leader of Protestant Europe in the great confrontation with the Spanish-Hapsburg powers, the threat of which loomed over Europe in the early years of the seventeenth century. We cannot quite know how this grave and secret young man proposed to deal with it. He certainly meant, unlike his father, to take a strong line. Whether he hoped through a great Protestant alliance – he was in contact with Christian of Anhalt and other European Protestant leaders[11] – to break the Hapsburg power and after having done so to end 'the jars in religion' through some wide-ranging solution, remains a question which his early death, and all those papers which he destroyed before his death, leaves unanswerable. Would Prince Henry, who might have seemed to enthusiasts something like a cross between Henry V and the Earl of Essex, have embroiled his father's 'Great Britain' in a war which would have destroyed it, as other European countries were to be destroyed in the Thirty Years' War? Or would he have taken action which would have averted that war and destroyed its causes, as some people – perhaps wrongly – believed possible? Prince Henry is a great historical question mark, comparable to another Henry, Henry of Navarre, that is Henri IV, King of France, whose assassination

1a   Prince Henry.
Miniature attributed
to Isaac Oliver.
Fitzwilliam Museum,
Cambridge

1b   Prince Henry.
Portrait attributed to
Robert Peake the
Elder.
Magdalen College,
Oxford

Erratum

Plate 2 should read: *Inigo Jones. St George's Portico, 'Prince Henry's Barriers'. Devonshire Collection, Chatsworth.*
and
Plate 3 should read: *Inigo Jones. Ruined Palace of Chivalry, 'Prince Henry's Barriers'. Devonshire Collection. Chatsworth.*

2   *Inigo Jones. Ruined Palace of Chivalry, 'Prince Henry's Barriers'.*
Devonshire Collection, Chatsworth

3   *Inigo Jones. St George's Portico, 'Prince Henry's Barriers'.*
Devonshire Collection, Chatsworth

4   *Inigo Jones. The Rock, 'Masque of Oberon'. Devonshire Collection, Chatsworth*

5 *Inigo Jones. Oberon's Palace. 'Masque of Oberon'. Devonshire Collection,*
Chatsworth

POLY-OLBION

GREAT BRITAINE

By
Michaell Drayton
Esqr:

London printed for   M Lownes. I Browne. I.Swaine
I Helme. I Busbie.

6   *Title-page, Michael Drayton,* Polyolbion, *London, 1612*

HENRICVS PRINCEPS

William Hole sculp:

7   *Prince Henry. Engraving in Michael Drayton,* Polyolbion,
London, 1612

NON SINE SOLE
IRIS

8   The 'Rainbow Portrait' of Queen Elizabeth I. Hatfield House

on 14 May 1610, on the eve of setting out for Germany on some great military enterprise, leaves unanswered the question of what exactly it was that he intended to do, and whether, if he had succeeded in doing it, the whole course of European history might have been different.

In fact, there is a close connection between the two question marks, for Henri IV was assassinated just one month before the young Prince Henry was created Prince of Wales. Henri IV had been the leader to whom the European liberals had been looking as the antidote to Hapsburg tyranny: James I of Great Britain had been in alliance with him. The death of Henri IV left a vacant place in the leadership into which it seemed possible that Prince Henry might step, young as he was, and for which he had possibly been preparing himself with serious purpose.

The conversion of Henry of Navarre had aroused widespread European hopes that some generous solution of the religious schism might be at hand, foreshadowed by the acceptance of the former Protestant leader into the Catholic church. Giordano Bruno had gone to Italy in 1592 hoping great things of the King of Navarre,[12] only to be thrown into the prisons of the Inquisition and later burned at the stake. In spite of set-backs of this kind, Europe in the early seventeenth century was still seething with hopes (notwithstanding the decrees of the Council of Trent) of some conciliatory solution of religious disunion. Prince Henry was not the only European who thought that ways might be found of ending the 'jars in religion', but it may be that the plan was first to break the intolerant Hapsburg powers by military intervention. This would be a different attitude from James I's policy of peace through appeasement.

The miniature of Prince Henry (Pl. 1a) attributed to Isaac Oliver, suggests a knight of romance, serious with the weight of destiny. The portrait at Magdalen College (Pl. 1b) shows him not long before his death, pale and drawn, muffled in the Garter robes. This sad figure, the focus of such tremendous hopes and aspirations, was about to slip out of life and out of history, his work undone.

The image of Prince Henry as a youth of destiny was built up in the new medium which Inigo Jones was popularising at the Stuart court, the masque. The early masques, or masque-like events, around Prince Henry took the form of chivalric exercises in romantic settings, and show clearly enough their continuity with the Elizabethan Accession Day Tilts, those knightly exercises of Eliza's reign.

Prince Henry was first brought significantly into public notice in January 1610, at the event known as 'Prince Henry's Barriers',[13] which took place in the Banqueting House at Whitehall. 'Barriers' are an exercise in which the knights fight on foot across a dividing bar.[14] Prince Henry's 'Barriers' were both a real martial exercise in which the Prince gave proof of his training in knightly activities, and a theatrical spectacle, or masque, written in verse by Ben Jonson, the theme of which related mythically to the young Prince in a setting designed by Inigo Jones. Two of Jones's existing masque designs belong to the setting for 'Prince Henry's Barriers'.

The first scene showed a ruined palace (Pl. 2) the dilapidated state of which alluded to the contemporary decay of chivalry. Ben Jonson's words in the opening scene of the masque explain the setting; it is the 'House of Chivalry' which 'decayed, or rather ruined, seems'. On the left is a tomb, the tomb of Merlin, symbolising the lost magic and learning in the palace of lost chivalry. But Merlin rises from his tomb and summons forth the hero who will restore chivalry to its former glory, Meliadus, Lord of the Isles, otherwise Prince Henry.

The scene now changed to one illustrating the revival or recovery of chivalry (Pl. 3). It showed 'St George's Portico', a gorgeous chapel dedicated to St George, the patron saint of England and of the Order of the Garter. In contrast to the dilapidation of the House of Chivalry in the previous scene, St George's Portico is resplendent and undamaged, and, to under-line the allusion, the maiden Chivalry, seen on the right issuing from a cave in which she has been imprisoned, awakes from sleep, inspired by the presence of Meliadus and his knights.

'Break, you rusty doors that have so long been shut', cries
Chivalry,

> and from the shores
> Of all the world come knighthood like a flood
> Upon these lists. . . .

These words announced the 'Barriers' in which Prince Henry
and his troop displayed their prowess and their grace.

Ben Jonson's words, in the speeches written for this show,
explain the meaning of the settings as referring to the decay of
chivalry and its restoration by Prince Henry, and they invest the
Prince and the King, his father, with all the romance of the
Tudor mythology. The speeches recall the days of King Arthur,
emperor over a united Britain. The story of the former greatness
of Arthur's court is told by the Lady of the Lake. Arthur himself
appears and proclaims the arrival of one greater than himself. A
prominent part in the dialogue is taken by the magician Merlin,
whose power is also reviving and whose prophecies are being
fulfilled.

James and his Queen and his other two children sat watching
the show. The role of a revived and greater Arthur was intended
primarily to refer to the King. He is hailed as the descendant of
Henry VII, who was really James's ancestor, and who, as a Tudor
king, passed on to him with the right to the throne of England
the whole Tudor panoply of the descent from the Trojan Brut
and from King Arthur.[15] Through Henry VII, James succeeds to
the traditions of Tudor rule as expressed in 'the great Eliza'.

These glories are carried on into the present generation by
Prince Henry, reviver of Chivalry and hero of the Barriers. He
will 'conclude all jars'; the spheres are now in tune again; in the
bright palace of St George's Portico Henry and his knights
appear, and the lady Chivalry is rescued from her cave. Merlin
reads the device on Henry's shield and recites the fame of his
British ancestors. Britain was 'the only name that made Caesar
fly'. Prince Henry's supposed resemblance to Henry V is
mentioned:

> Harry the fifth, to whom in face you are
> So like. . . .

Prince Henry is the successor to the glories of Agincourt and to the great victory in Eliza's time, the scattering of the Armada in 1588.

At the end, Merlin includes in his panegyric Henry's young brother (the future Charles I) and his sister, the Princess Elizabeth, sitting with their parents to watch the scene. The Princess's future marriage is referred to and a glorious destiny prophesied for her descendants:

> That most princely maid, whose form might call
> The world to war, and make it hazard all
> His valour for her beauty; she shall be
> Mother of nations, and her princes see
> Rivals almost of these. . . .

This prophecy was a little near the mark, since Elizabeth, as Queen of Bohemia, was to see the beginning of the Thirty Years' War, and her descendants were the Hanoverian kings of Great Britain.

Thus did Prince Henry begin his career on this world's stage, as a theatrical hero, heir to Brut and to the mythology of the British History, delivering Chivalry from a cave in the presence of his family.

The note struck by 'Prince Henry's Barriers' continues in the symbolism of the festivals up to and including the year of his death. It is a symbolism which gives prominence to the older generation – James must always receive chief honour as the monarch – but the second generation, the generation of his children, stand forth as the inheritors of the promise. Henry and Elizabeth, young people of striking character and handsome appearance, shine beside their parents as the hope of the future.

On 4 June 1610, Henry was created Prince of Wales. Since in the previous month, as already mentioned, Henri IV of France had been assassinated, the young Prince of Wales, with his known views and strong character, became a focus of interest both in Great Britain and in Europe generally. Part of the celebrations for his accession to the title of Prince of Wales consisted in a firework display. One contemporary states that almost half a million people watched this display.[16] The figure seems impossibly high and the statement may only mean that crowds unusually large for those times had gathered in London. What did those fireworks show in the night sky to those anxious crowds? There seems to be no description extant of the subject of these fireworks, but two years later, soon after Henry's death, the King's gunners gave a firework display in honour of his sister's betrothal to the Elector Palatine, the description of which has been preserved. The subject was St George as a knight of chivalry delivering a distressed maiden.[17] One wonders whether this show was a repetition of one in honour of Prince Henry. The appearance of St George, shining in the sky as a Red Cross knight, would certainly have suited the theme of the 'Barriers' in which the deliverers of Chivalry emerge from St George's Portico.

The themes of the 'Barriers' of January 1610 were continued in 'Oberon, The Fairy Prince', a masque in honour of Prince Henry given at court in January 1611, with words by Ben Jonson and scenery by Inigo Jones.[18] James was again the presiding King Arthur, and Prince Henry was Oberon, a fairy prince attended by fairy knights. The first scene showed a great rock (Pl. 4) which in the next scene opened to reveal a fairy palace (Pl. 5) of supposedly ancient British or Arthurian classical design.[19] Here was the home of Arthur's knights, once the noblest of the earth and now quickened by a second birth. The whole palace opened, discovering the 'nation of fays', and, afar off, the knights masquers, led by Oberon in a chariot.

Thus the theme of the revival of chivalry in the new generation – in the fairy prince, son of Arthur-James – is again set in the form of figures of romance emerging from rocks or caves. And the fairy imagery in 'Oberon' harks back to that of the 'Fairy Queen', to Eliza, heroine of the Spenserian romance of chivalry.

Once again, the new generation is seen as reviving the values of the Elizabethan past.

The source of the 'British' legend, of which the Tudors, and now the Stuarts, made such use was, of course, the famous *History of the Kings of Britain*, written by Geoffrey of Monmouth[20] in the twelfth century, which tells the exciting tale of how Brut, descendant of the Trojan Aeneas, came to the island of Albion and there founded the line of the British kings, culminating in King Arthur. The authenticity of Geoffrey's *History* had been questioned in the early sixteenth century by Polydore Vergil,[21] and other criticisms had been directed at it since then. It was, however, so necessary emotionally as the basis of the Tudor imperial legend, through which the Tudors were able to vie with other European dynasties in producing a descent from Troy,[22] that criticisms were ignored, and the 'British History' remained firmly enshrined in the Elizabethan imagination. With the growth of historical criticism, one might have expected the hold of the British legends to have weakened by the early seventeenth century, but, as we have seen, they were now applied to the Stuarts and so retained their strength and importance. The emphasis on legendary continuity of the new dynasty with the former reigning house helped to facilitate, emotionally, the transfer of loyalties.

The revival of the 'British History' in the displays at court in honour of Prince Henry had behind it a background of other contemporary efforts to connect the Stuarts with the Tudor myth. One of the most important of these was Michael Drayton's poem, *Polyolbion*,[23] a long account of the island of Albion, recently named 'Great Britain', its coasts, hills, cities, and, above all, its rivers. The poem is both topographical and historical, a loving description of the beauties of the wonderful island which also evokes its history. And the history of Albion is, for Drayton, the British History of Geoffrey of Monmouth.

The first part of *Polyolbion*, dedicated to Prince Henry, was published in 1612, the year of the Prince's death. The title-page (Pl. 6) shows Great Britain, a lady seated on an island in the ocean;

her robe is a map of her cities, streams, and forests. Around her stand her former rulers who are described in the poem facing the title-page. At the top left is Brut, described as the nephew of Aeneas. Brut carries a shield, the arms of which are not clear in the illustration, but the poem states that they are

> In Golden field the Lion passantred.

The lion was the heraldic animal of Brut, the British ancestor.[24] Facing Brut is Caesar, representing the Roman conquest of Britain and the Roman rule. Below Brut, the figure represents a Saxon and the Saxon rule; facing him is a Norman, introducing another dynasty. But now Great Britain has 'changed her love to him whose line yet rules'. This is the last line of the verses explaining the frontispiece, and it links the design with the reigning Stuarts, inheritors, like the Tudors, of the descent from Brut.

Turning over the frontispiece, we come on the next page to the dedication of the book to 'the High and Mightie Henrie, Prince of Wales', and, turning again, we find ourselves faced with an engraving of the Prince (Pl. 7). It shows Henry, the knight, his plumed helmet on the ground beside him, exercising at his military sports. This is the Henry of the 'Barriers' and of 'Oberon', the hope of the future, as the verses opposite proclaim:

> Britaine, behold here portray'd to thy sight
> Henry, thy best hope, and the world's delight.

Drayton dates the preface to his book May 1612. Six months later Britain's best hope and the world's delight would die.

The author of *Polyolbion*, leisurely and verbose, leads the reader on a conducted tour of Shakespeare's Albion, its plains, watered by many streams, its lovely wild flowers, its forests and hills, summoning up, as we follow him, its romantic legends and its 'British' History. For example, when the poet in his itinerary reaches Milford Haven, in Pembrokeshire, he expatiates on the fact that here landed Henry VII, the Tudor. And this, of course, involves him in British History, in the prophecy that the ancient

British race would return to rule in the Tudors, and then in the Stuarts.[25]

> . . . for thus the Powers reveale,
> That when the Norman Line in strength shall lastlie faile
> (Fate limiting the time) th' ancient Britan race
> Shall come againe to sit upon the soveraigne place,
> A branch sprung out of Brute, th' imperiall top shall get,
> Which grafted in the stock of great Plantaginet,
> The Stem shall strongly wax, as still the Trunk doth wither:
> That power which bare it thence, againe shall bring it thither
> By Tudor, with faire winds from little Britaine driven,
> To whom the goodlie Bay of Milford shall be given. . . .

The poet continues laboriously to connect this Tudor landing at Milford Haven with the 'Stewards' ' noble name, thus, through the common ancestor in Henry VII, connecting Stuarts with Tudors. Henry VII, and his landing at Milford Haven, was most important for the Stuart adaptation of the Tudor myth.

Printed with Drayton's *Polyolbion* are extremely learned prefaces and commentaries by John Selden, the antiquary. These are important since they discuss the Stuart adaptation of the 'British' myths in the light of contemporary antiquarian and historical research. Selden shows knowledge of the whole literature for and against the British History. As a scholar, he obviously doubts the Brut legend, but he allows it for its poetic truth, and defends and admires Drayton's Muse as she retells the ancient myths and elegantly connects them with the present royal line. The attitude is exactly the same as that of Ronsard, who in 1570 wrote an epic poem, *La Franciade*, in honour of Francus, the Trojan ancestor of the French kings, in whose real existence he did not believe but justified the use of the legend in patriotic poetry.[26]

Selden's notes deserve careful study. For example, in his commentary on the line

> To whom the goodlie Bay of Milford shall be given

he mentions the 'Eagle Prophecies'.[27] These were prophecies, supposedly uttered by an eagle, which are mentioned by Geoffrey of Monmouth, and were assumed, like the prophecies of Merlin, to belong to the prophetic preparation for the return of the British race in the Tudors.[28] Selden brings in the 'eagle pro-phecies' (which had been earlier mentioned by Drayton) in connection with Henry VII and his descendants, the Stuarts.

Drayton and his commentator are obviously very close in spirit to the masques at court before the death of Prince Henry. The maps which decorate *Polyolbion* are enlivened with graceful nymphs of rivers which may well recall the masque of 'Tethys' Festival', given at court in June 1610, on the occasion of the creation of Henry as Prince of Wales. The ladies of the court represented nymphs of English rivers (Princess Elizabeth was the Thames). The maps illustrating *Polyolbion*, with their nymphs in graceful dancing poses, must surely reflect the masque spirit, as do also Drayton's elaborate descriptions of the costumes worn by his river nymphs.

Drayton and Selden frequently echo Spenser. They belong to the spirit of Elizabethan revival around Henry and Elizabeth. The publication in 1612[29] of the poem marks it as one of the latest manifestations of the movement, so soon to be blighted by Henry's death.

The stresses and strains inherent in the difference between the outlook and policies of James and the hopes and enthusiasms of a large number of his subjects came out nowhere more visibly than in the marriage projects for his children. True to his policy of appeasement, James was bent on marrying one of them into the Spanish-Catholic side of the European divide and the other into the Protestant side. Projects for marrying Prince Henry to a Spanish princess, or a princess of the house of Savoy which was under Spanish influence, and the Princess Elizabeth to a Pro-testant prince, began to be canvassed from about 1604 onwards.[30] Henry appeared to be docile and ready to marry as his elders decided, though his friend Walter Raleigh argued strongly from his prison against a Spanish match.[31]

Evidence for the unpopularity of such a match can be gleaned from many quarters, and particularly from the play *Philaster* by Beaumont and Fletcher. This play was first referred to in 1610 (it was not printed until 1620).[32] It may therefore have been written at about the time of the coming into prominence of Prince Henry. There is a possible allusion in it to the ship being built for the Prince by Phineas Pett. This play is about a proposed Spanish match, favoured by a king who rules over two kingdoms, and who wishes to marry his daughter, Arethusa, to a Spanish prince. The match is strongly objected to by Philaster, who himself loves the princess. The situation is near, though not quite the same as that between James and his children; Philaster is not the brother of Arethusa. Nevertheless this contest between an older royal generation which wants a Spanish match and a younger generation which does not want it is sufficiently close to the contemporary situation to suggest that *Philaster* could belong to the world of the supporters of Prince Henry and of the revived Elizabethan type of chivalry which he represented.

The play *Philaster* is full of echoes of Philip Sidney, the hero of Elizabethan Protestant chivalry. The very name of the hero of the play is an allusion to Astrophel, lover of a star, which was Sidney's pseudonym. Moreover the style and the themes of *Philaster* constantly recall Sidney's romance, the *Arcadia*. The characters wander through pastoral landscapes exhibiting their romantic passions and their adherence to a Sidneian code of chivalric Puritanism. The exception is the Spanish prince, objected to by Arethusa and Philaster, who is lecherous and base. He has no difficulty in seducing the whore, Megra, and the unchastity of these two forms the foil to the star-like purity and integrity of Philaster and Arethusa. In the atmosphere of the times, of the anxious passions attendant on the proposed Spanish-Catholic marriages for James's children, the allusion would surely be obvious. The Spanish match meant encouragement of the Whore of Babylon. Philaster stood for Sidney and the Elizabethan chivalric tradition.

Prince Henry succeeded in eluding the Spanish match by

dying unmarried in 1612. But before that tragic event occurred the other half of his father's marriage policy, the marriage of his daughter to a Protestant prince, had taken shape.

The young Elector Palatine of the Rhine, chief lay elector of the Empire and head of the Union of German Protestant princes, landed at Gravesend on 16 October 1612, the betrothed of the Princess Elizabeth.[33] Prince Henry was deeply interested in the match, and was in touch with the activist Protestants who were pushing the policies of the Protestant Union. As he grew older, the Prince's opposition to a Spanish match for himself had stiffened. It was said that he intended to accompany his sister into Germany and to marry a German Protestant princess.[34] These important questions, so vital for Europe at this juncture, were presented in London in terms of romance. The Prince and his sister were tenderly attached to one another; the young Elector Palatine, a handsome youth, was in love with his beautiful betrothed. It was an Arcadian situation between brother and sister and lover, but the Arcadian theme, the aura of theatre and romance, concealed deadly realities, the realities of the contemporary European situation in which the Hapsburg powers were massing and the opposing side gathering together its forces. Most important for this situation was the question of what position James and 'Great Britain' would take.

On 17 November 1612, only one month after the arrival of the Elector Palatine, Prince Henry died at the age of nineteen. The Elector was about the same age; Princess Elizabeth a little younger. The group of young people, the hope of the future, had received a crushing blow. Their strongest member had been most suddenly and unexpectedly removed from this world's stage on which he had not yet played his part. His death was a disaster for the German Protestant policies, for the whole European movement of opposition to the Hapsburg powers. It frightened James, already very frightened by the Gunpowder Plot and by the death of Henri IV of France. Though foul play was suspected, it seems that the cause of the Prince's death was typhoid fever. His sudden disappearance was a shock from which vast enterprises, hanging in the balance, never recovered. It marked with a presage of disaster the hopeful marriage of his sister.

The preparations for the wedding went on after Henry's death, though the date was postponed. There was a betrothal ceremony, and finally on 14 February 1613, the wedding took place, in the chapel at Whitehall. The Protestant and religious aspect of the splendid occasion, attended by a brilliant gathering, was apparent to all. Archbishop Abbot, who performed the ceremony, regarded it as marking a high point for Anglican influence in Europe. The Palsgrave (as the Elector Palatine was called in England) spoke the words of the Anglican service in English. Though a German Calvinist, he was deeply in sympathy with Anglicanism and held many conferences with the Archbishop. The political aspect was emphasised by the fact that the Banqueting House at Whitehall was decorated with tapestries representing the defeat of the Spanish Armada. This reminder of the triumph of 1588, the glory of Eliza's reign, looked like a revival of Elizabethan leadership against Spain. The Spanish and Flemish ambassadors demonstrated their disapproval of the marriage by refusing to attend. Perhaps they knew of the rumours current in some quarters that supporters of this Anglo-Palatinate wedding entertained wild hopes of weakening the Hapsburg hold on the Empire.[35] There were many surmises circulating in Europe at this time of possible changes in the Empire following the death of Rudolph II in 1612. It was widely held that his death might open the door to apocalyptic changes.[36]

At any rate one thing seemed clear. With James at last marrying his daughter to the head of the Union of German Protestant Princes it looked as though he had finally made up his mind to support that side. Enthusiasts for the Elizabethan tradition were overjoyed.

The young bride was seen as a rebirth of the phoenix, a return to life of that phoenix, Queen Elizabeth I, and of all that she had represented. The symbols which had been used of Queen Elizabeth were showered on Princess Elizabeth, particularly the symbol of the phoenix. She was a phoenix bride, in whom the old Virgin Queen became young again, reborn as a bride. 'Up then, fair phoenix bride', cries John Donne in his 'Marriage Song on the Lady Elizabeth and the Count Palatine',[37] and he underlines the point that the phoenix bride is a rebirth of the old phoenix, Queen Elizabeth I. She signifies

> That a great princess falls, but doth not die.

The old queen lives again in this new Elizabeth for whom a great destiny is waiting.

Thus many hopes and allusions clustered round the figure of the young Elizabeth on her wedding day. As a pure bride, she also represented a pure church, a phoenix rebirth of Queen Elizabeth in this changed bridal form, an inheritor of religious-imperial destiny, and one for whom, perhaps, an even wider destiny than that of the Virgin Queen awaited.

According to one description of the wedding of Princess Elizabeth, the bride wore[38]

> a crown of refined golde, made imperiall by the pearls
> and diamonds thereupon placed, which were so thick
> beset that they stood like shining pinnacles upon
> her amber-coloured haire, dependently hanging playted
> downe over her shoylders to her waste.

There is a portrait, said to be of Queen Elizabeth I, which comes insistently into the memory as we think of Princess Elizabeth on her wedding day. It is the so-called 'Rainbow Portrait' at Hatfield House (Pl. 8). I have made various attempts in the past at studying this portrait, discussing the symbols of Queen Elizabeth I with which it is crowded,[39] and elucidating the strange head-dress as having been copied from an engraving illustrating a 'Thessalonian Bride'.[40] Within the head-dress, and not in the engraving from which it is copied, are jewels in the form of an imperial crown. I conjectured that the portrait might reflect some allegorical build-up of Queen Elizabeth I at an Accession Day Tilt. The gauntlet on the ruff suggests a chivalric setting.

The portrait has been tentatively dated 1600 (there is no date on it). The face is much too young for that of Queen Elizabeth at that date, and it would seem to have been copied from some 'young' representation of the Queen.[41]

An elaborate study of this portrait has since been made by René Graziani[42] in which he strongly emphasises the long hair of the sitter. Brides wore their hair long and this, coupled with the head-dress of the 'Thessalonian Bride', suggests to Graziani that this is a bridal portrait, which he interprets as religious allegory, relating to Queen Elizabeth I as the bride of Christ.

I now suggest that the 'Rainbow Portrait' may reflect Princess Elizabeth as a bride, with her hair hanging down. In this context it would still be understood as a 'young' Elizabeth I, reconstructed from a 'young' mask, but the reconstruction would refer to the rebirth of Queen Elizabeth in the young 'phoenix bride', wearing her bridal-imperial head-dress and gently displaying the Rainbow of Peace. The intensely religious character of the allegory would remain extremely apposite for Princess Elizabeth as a bride representing a pure church.

Laments for the death of Prince Henry mingled with the rejoicings over his sister's marriage, which was glorified by an extraordinary outpouring of dramatic art. On the night of the wedding a masque was presented with words by Thomas Campion and scenery by Inigo Jones,[43] with a wondrous presentation of the harmony of the spheres, alluding to the harmony to be established by this wedding, and including a solemn prophecy by a Sibyl of the Kings and Emperors who will arise from this union between Germany and Great Britain. The union of this pair represented the joining of the peoples in religious cult and in simple love. Perhaps something of the late Prince Henry's hopes for ending the 'jars in religion' entered into this masque. It may have presented a problem to the organisers of these festivities how to revise or omit allusions to the dead prince; the festivities had actually been ordered by Prince Henry himself[44] to grace his sister's wedding, and they had probably been prepared whilst he was still alive.

An extraordinary dramatic privilege accorded to the Elector Palatine and the Princess was that during the Christmas season of 1612 before their wedding, they saw a series of plays at court given by the King's Men, Shakespeare's company. Amongst these were six plays by Shakespeare, including two of the Last Plays, *The Winter's Tale* and *The Tempest*. It has been thought that the masque in *The Tempest* may have been added to an earlier version of the play to make it suitable for presentation before them.[45] Shakespeare himself was in London at the time.

In the following three lecture-chapters, it will be argued that the atmosphere of Elizabethan revival around the younger royal generation is the atmosphere to which Shakespeare's Last Plays belong. The events and movements which I have described, and, above all, the imagery accompanying them, can prove an essential guide to the meaning of the imagery in these plays.

Notes

1 *Astraea*, pp. 88 ff.
2 Ibid., pp. 69 ff.
3 D. H. Willson, *King James VI and I*, Cape, London, 1956, paperback, 1963, pp. 250–2.
4 Geoffrey Ashe, *The Quest for Arthur's Britain*, Paladin paperback, 1971, p. 20.
5 Peter French, *John Dee*, Routledge & Kegan Paul, London, 1972, p. 10.
6 Charles Cornwallis, *Discourse of Prince Henry, late Prince of Wales*, 1641; printed in John Somers, *Tracts*, II, 1809, pp. 217 ff.
7 *Calendar of State Papers, Venice, Vol. XII, 1610–1631* (despatches of Foscarini), pp. 194, 448 ff., etc.
8 Ibid., p. 450.
9 John Nichols, *The Progresses of James I*, II, 1826, p. 474; see *RE*, p. 2.
10 Cornwallis, p. 220; these were subjects taught in Dee's mathematical preface to Euclid, see *Theatre*, pp. 22–7; and by Robert Fludd, ibid., pp. 46–50.
11 See below, pp. 57–8.
12 *Bruno*, p. 340.
13 Stephen Orgel and Roy Strong, *Inigo Jones and the Theatre of the Stuart Court*, Sotheby, London, 1973, I, pp. 159–65; Ben Jonson, *Works*, ed. C. H. Herford and P. Simpson, Oxford University Press, 1937, VII.

14 *Tapestries*, p. 90 and Pl. VII.

15 T. D. Kendrick, *British Antiquity*, Methuen, London, 1950, pp. 34 ff.; *Astraea*, pp. 50 ff.

16 'A Relation of the Formalities and Shews made at the Creation of Henry Prince of Wales, on the 4th June 1610', in Ralph Winwood, *Memorials of Affairs of State in the Reigns of Q. Elizabeth and K. James I*, London, 1725, III, p. 181.

17 *RE*, pp. 3–4.

18 Orgel and Strong, I, pp. 205–16; Jonson, *Works*, VII.

19 *Theatre*, p. 175.

20 Geoffrey of Monmouth, *The History of the Kings of Britain*, trans. Lewis Thorpe, Penguin Books, 1966.

21 Kendrick, pp. 79 ff.; *Astraea*, pp. 50, 132.

22 The mythical Trojan ancestor of the Kings of France was Francus; see *Astraea*, p. 132 and Pl. 19a (representation of Francus at a French royal entry).

23 Michael Drayton, *Polyolbion*, in Michael Drayton, *Works*, ed. J. W. Hebel and K. Tillotson, Oxford University Press, 1961, IV.

24 The Lion arms of Brut were incorporated into the royal arms of Queen Elizabeth I; see Kendrick, *British Antiquity*, Pl. XI.

25 Drayton, *Works*, IV, p. 98.

26 *Astraea*, pp. 132–3.

27 Drayton, *Works*, IV, pp. 106–7.

28 Geoffrey of Monmouth, ed. cit., pp. 80, 283; cf. Thorpe's introduction, p. 23.

29 Drayton had been writing it for years before publication; see B. H. Newdigate, *Michael Drayton and his Circle*, Oxford University Press, 1961, pp. 158 ff.

30 Willson, pp. 282–3.

31 Walter Raleigh, 'A politique Discourse, by way of a Dispute about the happiest Marriage for the noble Prince Henry', printed in Somers, *Tracts*, II, pp. 199 ff.

32 Beaumont and Fletcher, *Philaster*, ed. Andrew Gurr, Methuen, London, 1969, Introduction, pp. xxvi ff.

33 For the betrothal, wedding, and festivities connected with these events, see Nichols, II, 1826; *RE*, pp. 2–7.

34 *Calendar of State Papers, Venice, Vol. XII*, p. 450.

35 A correspondent of Ralph Winwood's wrote to him from Brussels in March 1612, reporting that there is much talk in that city of 'our happy conjunction with the Palatinate; whereat these men [Catholics in Brussels] are enraged, fearing indeed thereby that we do aim at the wresting of the Empire out of the Austrian's hands' (Winwood, *Memorials*, III, p. 439).
    The Venetian ambassador in London noted as significant in May 1612, that in the present interregnum in the Empire, after the death of Rudolph, the Elector Palatine held the office of Imperial Vicar (*Calendar of State Papers Venice, Vol. XII*, p. 349). The rumours flying in Europe of approaching profound changes in the Empire after the death of Rudolph helped to

give a mysteriously prophetic 'imperial' significance to the Anglo-German wedding.

36 *RE*, pp. 16–17.
37 John Donne, 'Epithalamium, or Marriage Song on the Lady Elizabeth and the Count Palatine', *Poems*, ed. H. J. C. Grierson, Oxford University Press, 1912, I, pp. 127–31.
38 Nichols, pp. 542–3; cf. *RE*, p. 4.
39 'Allegorical Portraits of Queen Elizabeth I at Hatfield', Hatfield House Booklet, 1952, reprinted in *Astraea*, pp. 215–19.
40 'Boissard's Costume-Book and Two Portraits', *Journal of the Warburg and Courtauld Institutes*, XXII, 1959, reprinted in *Astraea*, pp. 220–1.
41 Roy Strong, *Portraits of Queen Elizabeth I*, Oxford University Press, 1963, pp. 84–5.
42 René Graziani, 'The "Rainbow Portrait" of Queen Elizabeth I and its Religious Symbolism', *Journal of the Warburg and Courtauld Institutes*, XXXV, 1972, pp. 247–59.
43 Thomas Campion, 'The Lords' Masque'; Orgel and Strong, I, pp. 241–52; *RE*, pp. 5–6.
44 See below, p. 58.
45 *The Tempest*, ed. F. Kermode, Arden edition paperback, 1964, Introduction, pp. xxii–xxiii.

2

Cymbeline

Cymbeline, first printed in the Folio of 1623, was rather curiously grouped by the editors with the tragedies, though it has a happy ending. It is a strange play, a masque-like romance, or, if we are to call it a history, it is a 'British History'. The titular hero, King Cymbeline, occurs in Geoffrey of Monmouth's *History of the Kings of Britain* as one of King Arthur's predecessors on the British throne, in times before the conquest of Britain by the Romans.[1] Another such early British king was King Lear, the story of whom and of his three daughters, very briefly told by Geoffrey, lit up Shakespeare's imagination with such astounding results. Cymbeline had two sons, Guiderius and Arviragus; their legend, based on Geoffrey's story, is told by Holinshed with some variations. These two sons were war-like youths who resisted the Romans and refused to pay them tribute. Shakespeare used the names of Cymbeline and of his two valiant sons, just as he used the names of Lear and his three daughters, and allowed his imagination to play very strangely around them.

The really significant thing about King Cymbeline was, that according to Geoffrey, his reign in Britain synchronised with the reign of Caesar Augustus in Rome, and therefore it was in his time that Christ was born. As Spenser puts it, as he repeats the names of the kings in the British History:[2]

Next him *Tenantius* raigned, then Kimbeline
 What time th' eternall Lord in fleshly slime
 Enwombed was, from wretched *Adams* line
 To purge away the guilt of sinfull crime:
 O ioyous memorie of happy time,
 That heauenly grace so plenteously displayd;
 (O too high ditty for my simple rime).
 Soone after this the *Romanes* him warrayd;
For that their tribute he refused to be let payd.

This passage is the germ of *Cymbeline*, both of the basic elements
in a story found in the British History and of its spiritual meaning.
That meaning is concerned with new spiritual revelations, new
intimations of the divine, occurring in the reign of the British
king. Shakespeare had already seized on the Lear story as vehicle
of a vast spiritual drama. The Cymbeline story lent itself more
obviously to the expression of intimations from the spiritual
world, to the breaking through of some new Christ-like
revelation.

Shakespeare was drawing on those lines of thinking in the
traditional interpretation of the idea of Empire through which
the Roman Empire was sanctified and Christianised because
Christ chose to be born during the reign of Augustus Caesar.
The universal imperial *justitia* and *pax* was sanctified through that
birth, and through the interpretation of the prophecy in Virgil's
Fourth Eclogue as applying both to the peace and justice of the
Augustan golden age, and to the birth of Christ, the Prince of
Peace, in that age.[3] This Christianised interpretation of Empire.
and the symbolism accompanying it, had been extremely well
known in Tudor England, where it had formed an integral part
of the propaganda for the Monarch as having effected the reform
of the Church. Queen Elizabeth I's name of 'Astraea', the Virgin
Justice who reigned in the golden age, referred to her, not only
as a just ruler in the temporal sense, but as the just imperial
ruler, longed for by Dante, who had reformed the Church.[4] The
interpretation of the reign of Cymbeline as contemporary with

the reign of Augustus, in which Christ was born, gave it an atmosphere of the sacred; it approximated the British sacred reign to the sacred reign of Augustus Caesar; it drew together British imperial and Roman imperial sacred legend in some new fusion of Britain and Rome. This is exactly what happens in *Cymbeline* which is dominated by a vision of a Romano-British imperial eagle.

That Shakespeare's view of society is bound up with his belief in kingship as the principle of order, the divinely ordained channel for maintaining a just order on earth corresponding to the divine rule of the cosmos, is one of the most obvious and incontrovertible aspects of his outlook on life. And that Shakespeare's view of kingship extends beyond the merely national into vast vistas of universal spiritual order, or disorder, is clearly intimated in his imagery. It is thus natural and right to speak of an 'imperial theme' in connection with Shakespeare, and *The Imperial Theme* is in fact the title of a well-known book by G. Wilson Knight[5] which discusses Shakespeare's imagery of kingship, the divine and cosmic majesty with which he invests the kingly office, the striking descriptions of the lapse into chaos and confusion – tempest and disorder in the cosmos, tempest and disorder in the state – when the kingly office fails. It seems to be less well known to students of Shakespeare that this imagery of empire in its sacred aspects was the basis of the Tudor propaganda, the root of the symbolism used of Queen Elizabeth I in portraits and pageantry. These images of universally pure, or universally impure empire were raised in the propaganda of Shakespeare's time and in connection with the reform of the Church. And one of the main propaganda vehicles of the Tudor reform of the Church was through the appeal to British History, to Arthurian legend and its expression in chivalry, in the mission of knights to spread a pure spiritual order throughout the world, as described in Spenser's *Faerie Queene*.[6] Shakespeare had been confronted with such issues throughout his life, and had confronted them, sometimes with hope and sometimes with despair, in tragedies and histories. In *Cymbeline* he confronts the sacred imperial theme once more, in a last play, and after the despair of *Hamlet*, *Macbeth*, or *Lear*, he would seem to arrive in *Cymbeline* at some kind of solution, deriving both from some new historical situation, or new manifestation of the royal, but also, and mainly, from some new spiritual experience, new manifestation of the divine, which turned despair into a distant hope, a hope connected with King Cymbeline and particularly with his children, a hope that, perhaps after all, all was not lost, that in the generations to come all might yet be well. This, at least, is my reading of the inner meaning of the play, or of one of its meanings.

Read literally, *Cymbeline* is a tissue of impossible events and situations. The scene opens in Cymbeline's palace in Britain, where we learn from the conversation of courtiers that Imogen, the King's daughter, has just married against her parents' will an admired gentleman of the name of Posthumus Leonatus, or the lion-hearted, a name which has been conferred on him for glorious deeds; Posthumus Leonatus is to be banished for having married Imogen. The Queen, an evil woman, has an unpleasant son by a former marriage called Cloten whom she tries to force on Imogen. There is a sad parting scene between Imogen and Posthumus who leaves Britain for Rome.

The plot is now complicated by the introduction of a story about a wager, the gist of which Shakespeare had found in Boccaccio or in one of his imitators. When in Rome, Posthumus boasts to his acquaintances there about the chastity and virtue of his lady. The wicked Iachimo disbelieves him and wagers that he will prove that Imogen is unchaste and unfaithful. Posthumus accepts the wager. Iachimo goes to Britain, introduces himself to Imogen as her husband's friend, and asks her to take care of a chest which he says contains plate for the emperor. Imogen accepts the charge of the chest which is put into her bedchamber. It contains Iachimo, who emerges from it in the night whilst she is sleeping. He steals a bracelet from her arm, takes careful note of all the pictures and furniture in her room, and of a mole under her breast. With all these details, he later convinces Posthumus that the chaste Imogen has been false to him, that he, Iachimo, has had no difficulty in entering her room and seducing her. Posthumus loses faith in Imogen whom he now believes to be no better than a whore.

Driven from the court by the machinations of the wicked Queen and the hateful Cloten, Imogen dresses as a boy and flees. She finds refuge in a cave in Wales where Belarius, an exiled courtier, has reared two young boys. These boys are really King Cymbeline's sons who had been kidnapped and were believed dead, lost to the world for years and hidden in their cave. The boys do not know their birth, that they are the British princes, Guiderius and Arviragus, sons of Cymbeline. Imogen, whom they believe to be a boy and welcome to their cave, is really their sister. Cloten, pursuing Imogen, arrives at the cave and is killed by one of the boys. Imogen had been given by the wicked Queen a potion which the Queen believed to be a deadly poison but which had really been changed into a sleeping draught. Imogen takes it, falls asleep, and appears to be dead, to the great grief of Belarius and the young princes. She wakes to life again on the corpse of Cloten, a scene so strange that it seems to demand some allegorical explanation.

Meanwhile, the Romans have landed at Milford Haven to invade Britain, led by a good Roman called Lucius. Posthumus is with them as a prisoner but manages to join the British army which is defending Britain. The young British princes greatly distinguish themselves in the wars with the Romans. And Posthumus has in his sleep a remarkable vision, which has seemed to the many severe critics of this play its final ineptitude.

To the sound of solemn music, the ghosts of Posthumus's parents and brothers appear and warn him, in strangely archaic verses, not to believe Iachimo's slander of Imogen. They pray earnestly to Jupiter to descend to the aid of Posthumus. Jupiter descends, sitting on an eagle. He makes a speech promising that Posthumus shall be reunited to Imogen, and then ascends back to his crystalline palace in the heavens. Posthumus, on waking from his visionary sleep, finds a book on the ground containing a prophecy:[7]

When as a lion's whelp shall, to himself unknown,
without seeking find, and be embrac'd by a tender
piece of air: and when from a stately cedar shall be
lopp'd branches, which, being dead many years, shall
after revive, be jointed to the old stock, and freshly
grow, then shall Posthumus end his miseries, Britain
be fortunate, and flourish in peace and plenty.

The story proceeds to a happy ending; Posthumus and Imogen
are reunited; the evil characters are disposed of; even Iachimo
has confessed his knavish tricks and confirms that Imogen is purity
and chastity itself. The young British princes have covered themselves with glory in the wars against the Romans. They are
revealed to Cymbeline as his long-lost sons. Cymbeline presides
over a grand reunion of the family – two sons, a daughter, and
a son-in-law – in which the good Roman, Lucius, joins with the
Britons in peace and harmony. And the soothsayer, Philarmonus,
is called upon to interpret the prophecy, which he does as
follows:[8]

> Thou, Leonatus, art the lion's whelp,
> The fit and apt construction of thy name,
> Being Leo-natus, doth impart so much:
> (*To Cymbeline*) The tender piece of air, thy virtuous
>   daughter . . .
> The lofty cedar, royal Cymbeline,
> Personates thee: and thy lopp'd branches point
> Thy two sons forth: who, by Belarius stol'n,
> For many years thought dead, are now reviv'd,
> To the majestic cedar join'd; whose issue
> Promises peace and plenty. . . .

In this atmosphere of universal harmony, Cymbeline submits to
Caesar and promises to pay the tribute. The soothsayer avers
that:[9]

> The fingers of the powers above do tune
> The harmony of this peace.

He sees the Roman eagle spreading his wings from south to west, foreshadowing that[10]

> Th' imperial Caesar should again unite
> His favour with the radiant Cymbeline,
> Which shines here in the west.

Cymbeline ordains sacrifices to the gods and that the peace is to be proclaimed:[11]

> Publish we this peace
> To all our subjects. Set we forward: let
> A Roman and a British ensign wave
> Friendly together: so through Lud's town march,
> And in the temple of great Jupiter
> Our peace we'll ratify: seal it with feasts,
> Set on there! Never was a war did cease
> (Ere bloody hands were wash'd) with such a peace.

A vast Romano-British *pax* is being proclaimed, ratified with ceremonies and feasts in Lud's town (London), and the achievement of this *pax*, after misunderstanding and conflict, is the theme of the play.

The masque-like quality of *Cymbeline* has long been recognised but it has not been realised that the approach through masque and pageantry in the early years of the seventeenth century can tell us more about the meaning of *Cymbeline* than can the purely literary approach. We have seen that the Stuart inheritance of the Tudor myth was the theme of the performances at court in 1610 and 1611 in honour of Prince Henry. To James, the Stuart king, were now applied the legends of the British History. As a new Arthur, ruling over a new Great Britain, James presided over the shows in which his son and heir, Prince Henry, was being brought to the fore as the reviver of chivalry. In the 'Barriers' of 1610 this idea was presented through scenery representing a ruined Palace of Chivalry, restored in the next scene by the vision of St George's Portico, near which was a cave in which Chivalry was sleeping, but is restored to life by Henry's prowess in the barriers. In the following year, 1611, this symbolism was repeated in the form of scenes representing rocks which open to reveal, concealed within them as in a cave, the palace of Oberon, with Prince Henry with his knights-masquers again leading the revival of chivalry. King James as the new Arthur sat watching, on both occasions, the scenic presentation of Prince Henry as reviver of chivalry revealed by the opening of caves and rocks. The young prince for whom a great destiny appeared to be waiting in these early years of the century was presented to the public in this dream-like setting of masques based on the British History, the promise of which has descended, through Arthur-James, to his son. Not only Henry was honoured in these masques; the King's second son, Charles, was also present and was associated with his brother's heroic exploits. And his daughter, Elizabeth, sat with her parents to watch the shows, hailed in Ben Jonson's verses as the mother of future royal lines.

We know that a version of Shakespeare's *Cymbeline* was performed in 1611, for Simon Forman saw it then and recorded its plot. The details of this which Forman gives make it certain that it was a version of Shakespeare's play which he saw in 1611, and, surely, at that date, the spectacle of young British princes rescuing Chivalry from a cave, or issuing forth from rocks and caves in which they were hidden to revive Chivalry by their valour, must have reminded spectators of the great contemporary theme, Prince Henry, and his young brother, Prince Charles, the hope of the future, the reviver of chivalry. Their sister, Elizabeth, whose marriage was already being planned, was present at the shows in honour of her brother.

The editor of *Cymbeline* in the New Arden edition is uninterested in its obvious connections with the British History but other critics have been aware that such allusions were topical because of the Stuart adoption of the Tudor mythology. Emrys Jones in an article on 'Stuart Cymbeline' notes that the Tudor British myth was used to establish James in the line of the British kings; he thinks that the character of Cymbeline in the play has a direct reference to James and he notes that Shakespeare gives him two sons and a daughter, corresponding to James's actual family.[12] Bernard Harris, in an essay of 1967, agrees that the play has a topical theme, and he suggests that the marriage of the Princess Elizabeth with a Protestant hero might have been a suitable occasion for the revival of Tudor-British themes as applied to the Stuarts.[13] Bernard Harris's essay may be moving in the right direction but he does not go far enough in examining the British History themes in the play and their connection with contemporary situations.

These critics do not use the imagery of Prince Henry's masques to support their arguments. The masques have been used for comparison with the play, but only as arguing a possible influence of masque-stagecraft on Shakespeare, and without discussion of their meaning. Yet surely the masque scenery suggests, not only the actual scenic setting, but the meaning of that cave in Wales in which Guiderius and Arviragus were hidden, sons of King Cymbeline who issue from their cave to do chivalrous battle with Britain's enemies. The masques, it will be remembered, belonged to the glorification of Henry as Prince of Wales. Shakespeare's cave in Wales is surely a suitable scenic hiding-place for a Prince of Wales.

One of the most significant of the names of the characters in *Cymbeline* is the name, Imogen, of its heroine. It has been noticed by Emrys Jones and others, though not sufficiently emphasised, that this name connects directly with the British History. Imogen, or rather 'Innogen', as Forman spells it,[14] was a very suitable name for a young British princess, expected to be the ancestress of a royal line, for this name, in a slightly different spelling, is given in Geoffrey of Monmouth's *History of the Kings of Britain* as the name of the wife of Brut, the Trojan ancestor of the British kings.[15] Spenser, when resuming Geoffrey's *History* in the *Faerie Queene*, does not forget that the name of Brut's wife is 'Innogen'.[16] That the central character, and the most attractive character, in Shakespeare's play should bear the name of Imogen is surely an indication of how strongly the British History was present in Shakespeare's mind as he wrote it.

Why does Shakespeare give Imogen's husband the peculiar name of 'Posthumus Leonatus'? This riddle, too, can be solved if one remembers that the husband of 'Innogen' in the British History is Brut himself, the Trojan ancestor. Traditionally, the heraldic animal of Brut was said to be a lion, the British Lion.[17] And Geoffrey of Monmouth states that Brut's mother died in giving him birth.[18] He could therefore well be described as a Posthumous Lion, or Posthumus Leonatus. In the vision seen by Posthumus Leonatus in his sleep, an episode which seems somehow central to Shakespeare's meaning in the play, the ghosts of his ancestors and relatives utter a prophecy in strange archaic language.[19] These prophetic ghosts would be Trojans, uttering their prophecy of the return of the British line to rule. Shakespeare associates this prophecy with a vision of an eagle, and this again connects the scene with British History traditions, for Geoffrey of Monmouth speaks of an eagle prophecy which will be fulfilled when the British line returns to power.[20]

From the 'cave in Wales', Imogen makes her way towards Milford Haven where her husband, Posthumus, is expected to land. Why Milford Haven? Because, as Emrys Jones points out, it was there that Henry VII landed, the Tudor ancestor of James I, the ancestor through whom he could be connected with the Tudor mythology of the descent from the Trojan Brut.

It has already been shown that the topographical poem, *Polyolbion*, by Shakespeare's friend, Michael Drayton, is important for the elucidation of the use of British History in the masques in honour of Prince Henry. It is also very important for the elucidation of *Cymbeline*. Published in 1612, the year of Prince Henry's death, its frontispiece with a portrait of Brut and its engraving of Prince Henry at his martial sports show that this book belongs to the very heart of the movement associating Tudor and Stuart legend to which both the Prince Henry masques and Shakespeare's play belong. *Polyolbion* is a topographical, or choreographical, poem, extolling the beauties of Albion, and

exploring the island's legends. Written by a patriotic believer in
the British History, this poetic tour of Albion, with John Selden's
learned notes on it, represents the type of British antiquarian
research brought up to date in its topical allusions to James and
his son which lay behind the masques in honour of Prince Henry
and also behind *Cymbeline*. There is something of the air of a
topographical itinerary in Shakespeare's play, with its 'cave in
Wales' and its emphasis on 'Milford Haven'. In *Polyolbion*, too,
Wales is important and the significance of Milford Haven in
Tudor-Stuart legend is not forgotten, as has already been emphasised.[21] Leading features in *Cymbeline* – the mention of Milford
Haven and of Wales, the eagle prophecy – can be usefully illu-
minated by the British antiquarianism of *Polyolbion* and its
learned commentator. Shakespeare's imagination was moving
along the lines of a tour of Albion leading to Milford Haven,
an Albion soaked in the traditions of the British History,
brought up to date through allusion to the modern royal
Britons.

Drayton mentions the name of 'Bright Innogen',[22] who was
given to the 'noble Brut' as his wife. Voyaging with her over
strange seas, the Trojan ancestor eventually reached the Isle of
Albion, indicated by the goddess Diana as the land where he
should plant his Trojan race.[23]

> Where from the stock of Troy, those puissant kings
>   should rise
> Whose conquests from the West, the world should scant
>   suffice.

Surely, in choosing the name, Imogen, for his heroine, Shakespeare was attaching his play to the British legends, and indicating
that the Tudor-Stuart line might still be fertile in royal descendants. If the youths in the cave called to mind Prince Henry and
his brother, would not Imogen call to mind their sister, the
Princess Elizabeth, expected to be the 'mother of nations'?

Cymbeline fits perfectly well as a play produced about 1611 – the
play which Forman saw in 1611 – reflecting the glorification of

James and his children as inheritors of the Tudor mythology in the Prince Henry masques.

And it would fit still better as a play of 1611 revised in 1612 to allude to the coming marriage of the Princess Elizabeth to the Elector Palatine, with his German imperial associations. The prophecies of imperial destiny for the descendants of Brut would then include even wider associations through the marriage of the British Imogen with the senior lay Elector of the Holy Roman Empire. The lion was also the heraldic animal of the Palatinate, perhaps making possible his assimilation to Brut and the British lion,[24] and thus furnishing a second leonine allusion for Posthumus Leonatus.

I suggest that *Cymbeline* was written about 1611 when the masques were building up the British History in relation to James and his children, and that it was revised in 1612 to make it fit the rejoicings over Princess Elizabeth's engagement but *before the death of Prince Henry*. In this form it would have been a play fitted to reflect both the valorous personality of the living Prince Henry and the marriage of his sister to the Elector Palatine. When, at the end of *Cymbeline*, King Cymbeline-James presides over a family consisting of two sons, a daughter, and a son-in-law, the play would reflect a moment in the history of James's family before the death of Henry but after it became certain that Elizabeth would marry the Elector Palatine, that is a moment late in 1612, when poets, playwrights, masque-writers, were busy preparing their works in celebration of Princess Elizabeth's coming marriage.

A revealing comparison which can be made between *Cymbeline* and another contemporary work is the comparison with the masque which Thomas Campion wrote for the wedding, with production by Inigo Jones.[25] In this, the poetry combined with elaborate scenic effects to express the harmony of the spheres blending with the harmony of the royal wedding. The Rhine joins with the Thames; Germany unites with Great Britain. The peoples are joined in one religious cult and in simple love, and 'Old Sybilla' advances to prophesy in mystic verses the great race of kings and emperors which will spring from this union. The performance is close to the atmosphere of *Cymbeline* with its dreams and visions. Philarmonus, the soothsayer in *Cymbeline*, interprets the mysterious prophecy in terms of universal harmony; he is something like the presenter of a nuptial masque, a masque similar in atmosphere to others presented in honour of Princess Elizabeth's wedding. In *Cymbeline*, Shakespeare has combined his reflections of the Prince Henry type of masque, with chivalrous youths issuing from caves, with themes which might verge on a nuptial masque for his sister. The combination of masque-like presentation of Prince Henry and his brother with masque-like effects for their sister does not, perhaps, fuse quite satisfactorily. The boys in the cave are too young; the eldest boy does not quite represent the adult Prince Henry as he was at the time of his sister's engagement. Shakespeare did not have time to rewrite the whole play; he had to use the 1611 version, adding to its British imperial visions suggestions of the further destiny of the British Imogen through her marriage to a representative of the Holy Roman Empire.

The altering of plays and masques to suit changing circumstances may have been quite an industry in these years 1610 to 1612 when the pattern of events shifted so rapidly. A play written in *circa* 1611 to fit Prince Henry and Princess Elizabeth as they were then has to be adapted in 1612 to fit what was now known about Princess Elizabeth's future husband. One thinks of the nuptial masque in *The Tempest* which critics have thought may have been added to a 1611 version of the play to make it suitable for performance before Elizabeth and the Elector Palatine late in 1612, when they were betrothed.[26] It is thus not impossible that some adaptation of the *Cymbeline* of 1611 might have been made. Why, then, was such an adapted *Cymbeline* not acted before Elizabeth and the Palatine, as *The Tempest* was? Because, I suggest, Prince Henry and his plans were so deeply built into *Cymbeline* that the Prince could not be removed without wrecking the play, and the Prince was dead.

Thus, according to the approach attempted here, *Cymbeline*

would reflect the time just before Prince Henry's death when great adventures were planned by the Prince, acting in concert with his sister's future husband. After some bold, successful venture of a military character, a wide solution of universal peace would be established, an ending of the 'jars' in religion. The procession at the end of *Cymbeline* which goes to give thanks in Lud's Town for the conclusion of peace is led by King Cymbeline-James followed by his family, two sons, a daughter, and a son-in-law – and by the defeated and converted Roman leader. This great peace is not King James's idea of a peace of appeasement through marrying one half of his family into the Spanish-Hapsburg side. It is Prince Henry's idea of a peace to be achieved through defeating that side and afterwards arranging a universal religious peace, an ending of all religious jars.

Why did Shakespeare choose Cymbeline as the prototype of James, rather than Arthur, the British hero who represented the Stuarts in the contemporary propaganda? There may have been a reason, namely that Cymbeline was an early Briton who, with his sons, resisted the Romans, whereas Arthur, living in the age after the withdrawal of Roman rule, defended Roman traditions. The Cymbeline royal party are resisting Roman interference, though they expect an ultimate reconciliation when the tyranny has been broken. Drummond of Hawthornden said that he wished that 'Prince Henry had died in the act of conquering Rome'.[27] James's solution of peace through a Spanish match would not fit with this outlook.

In fact, *Cymbeline* may reflect the popular opposition to a Spanish match. This play is suffused with the influence of Sidney's *Arcadia* and has close connections with the play *Philaster* by Beaumont and Fletcher.[28] We have seen that the Beaumont and Fletcher play reflects opposition to the Spanish match in its story of a princess whom her parents wish to marry to a wicked and lascivious Spaniard, who is contrasted with the pure Philaster, inheritor of the Sidney tradition. The atmosphere of Arcadian romance which suffuses *Philaster* is also the atmosphere of *Cymbeline*, which shows strongly either a direct influence from *Philaster* or an indebtedness to the same Sidneian and Arcadian tradition. The opposition to a Spanish match in *Philaster* made it a suitable play to present before Princess Elizabeth and the Elector Palatine in 1612, and it was so presented, twice.[29] The chastity-before-marriage theme in *Philaster* should be compared with the same theme in *The Tempest*, where Prospero makes a great point of this in his admonitions to Ferdinand. When these two plays were acted before the royal couple, the point would surely have been obvious in the context of the times, when the hatred of a Spanish match, with its encouragement of a supposedly impure religion, was compared with the popularity of a pure Protestant match. The machinations against Imogen in *Cymbeline* might have, in the context of this general atmosphere, a suggestion of 'Popish plots', very much in the air since the Gunpowder Plot, success-fully eluded by the successful conclusion of the Protestant marriage.

Imogen, by far the most attractive and interesting character in *Cymbeline*, has been described by Wilson Knight as representing 'Britain's soul integrity',[30] a description which might have been strengthened by the recognition of her British name, Innogen, wife of Brut, the founder of the British-Trojan legend. We should expect a heroine with such a name to represent something like Britain's soul integrity, and the religious associations surrounding Imogen are brought out in the imagery. Imogen is both a beautiful and chaste woman and a pure reformed church. Imogen's bed-chamber contains pictures of 'chaste Dian' bathing, whilst its roof[31]

> With golden cherubins is fretted.

It is a church, a pure British church, which its enemies slander as impure. The misunderstandings between Imogen and Posthu-mus were due to slanderous misrepresentations by another church of the Imogen-church. But all is to be healed in a new imperial peace, a new outpouring of the divine in the holy reign of Cymbeline-Augustus-James.

This soothsaying seems confirmed when we remember that

Princess Elizabeth was seen as a newly reborn Queen Elizabeth I, representing like her the purity of a reformed church, inheriting her symbolism. Whether or not the 'Rainbow Portrait' alludes to Princess Elizabeth it can be used as a visual suggestion of how the Virgin Queen's image might be transformed into a bridal image. Imogen, too, would be a phoenix rebirth of the Elizabeth-image as a church, but now taking the form of a bride. And it is significant that Elizabeth symbols are used of Imogen, particularly the phoenix symbol. She is described as[32]

alone th' Arabian bird.

Without pressing this argument too far, it can surely be suggested that the line of approach to the imagery of the Imogen-church through the revival of Elizabeth-symbolism for Princess Elizabeth is revealing.

Also significant for Imogen, is the imagery used by John Donne in his 'Marriage Song on the Lady Elizabeth and the Count Palatine'.[33] It begins with an outburst of bird song, filling all the air, and comparable to the bird symbolism which has been noted as a feature of *Cymbeline*,[34] and to the curious description of Imogen in the prophecy as a 'tender piece of air'. Air is evidently the element of the Princess Elizabeth, and the chorus of birds the expression of her happiness. Above all, cries Donne, the phoenix is her bird. She is the old phoenix, Queen Elizabeth I, reborn as a 'fair phoenix bride'. Her marriage to the Palatine is a union of 'two phoenixes'.

> Up then, fair phoenix bride, frustrate the sun;
>   Thyself from thine affection
>   Takest warmth enough, and from thine eye
> All lesser birds will take their jollity.
>   Up, up, fair bride, and call
> Thy stars from out their several boxes, take
> Thy rubies, pearls, and diamonds forth, and make
> Thyself a constellation of them all;
>   And by their blazing signify

That a great princess falls, but doth not die.
Be thou a new star, that to us portends
Ends of great wonder; and be thou those ends.

This is the mood of *Cymbeline*, with its phoenix bride, Imogen, and its image of the eagle spreading its wings far and wide and promising a vast imperial destiny. Perhaps Shakespeare, too, hoped, as many did, that the Empire itself might eventually fall to the Palatine, that a universal imperial reform, solving all religious difficulties, might be the outcome of this wedding.

Such, in broad outline, is the new approach to *Cymbeline* suggested here. It is not a mere hypothesis put forward in a vacuum, and to be argued for and against, but an approach using new lines of historical and comparative material which can be further developed through future work along the lines suggested.

Basically, the approach is historical, concerned with a historical situation which is not well known, the rise to prominence of Prince Henry and Princess Elizabeth in the early years of the reign of James I, the hopes associated with these young people of the new generation by many, at home and abroad. I do not know of any adequate modern historical treatment of this theme. Owing to Prince Henry's early disappearance, he disappears also from history. Princess Elizabeth and her husband became engulfed in terrible disasters and disappeared into the confusion of the Thirty Years' War. To reconstruct the time when the young people were surrounded by hopes we have to go back to contemporary sources.

A good way of getting back into the atmosphere of the years in which Shakespeare wrote his last plays is to read straight through the *Calendar of Venetian State Papers* for the years 1610 to 1613, where all the events are recorded, interspersed with wise comments by the Venetian ambassadors who are watching events in London from a European point of view. In September 1610, we hear that the young Prince Palatine is thought to be a youth of remarkable qualities and suitable for Princess Elizabeth.[35] In November 1610, Christian of Anhalt, the German Protestant leader, arrives in London. He is urging King James to join the Union of Protestant Princes, and probably he will touch on the marriage of the Princess Elizabeth with the Palatine.[36] In January 1611, the Venetian ambassador saw Prince Henry's masque and greatly admired it, and the grace of the Prince's movements.[37] In May 1611, the ambassador attended a great ceremony of the Order of the Garter, at which the late Henri IV of France was honoured and mourned by Prince Henry.[38] In August 1611, he attends on Prince Henry and finds Maurice, Landgrave of Hesse, with him, an indication of the Prince's interest in the German Protestant movement. The Prince's aims are said to be very lofty.[39] Negotiations are rumoured in September for marrying the Prince to a Spanish princess, and for marrying the Princess Elizabeth to a member of the House of Savoy.[40] These rumours are unpopular with the people, and in January 1612, the preachers are touching on the marriages in the pulpits, praying that the Prince and Princess may not be married to Catholics, but to 'princes of this religion'.[41] Yet in February 1612, a Spanish match for the Princess Elizabeth is still rumoured,[42] though it is also said that the Duc de Bouillon, the French Protestant leader, is coming to conclude the match between her and the Palatine. He comes, and has a solemn audience with the King and Queen, seated on two thrones, with their children, Henry and Elizabeth, standing behind them.[43] Elizabeth's marriage with the Palatine has been concluded.[44] In September the arrival of the Palatine is expected, but is delayed because of plotting in the Spanish embassy in London.[45] The Spaniards are rumoured to be 'scattering pensions',[46] and Jesuits come and go at the embassy. Archbishop Abbot is alarmed about these movements of the Jesuits.[47] Finally, by 30 October, the Palatine has arrived at Dover, festivals are being prepared, crowds are coming to London.[48] On 9 November the Palatine and the Princess meet.[49] Sumptuous entertainments for their wedding are being ordered by Prince Henry.[50] A day or two later, Prince Henry is ill.[51] On 16 November he is very ill.[52] On 17 November he dies. The Venetian ambassador is profoundly grieved.[53] Amongst his comments are the following remarks: This prince was nearer to taking action than many thought. He is to be compared to Henri IV of France. He had intended to go into Germany with his sister. He had vast designs. He lent fire to the King, his father, in the affairs of Germany, aspired to be the head of the confederation of Protestant princes.[54] His death is a fearful loss, but nevertheless the world goes on. The Palatine is invested with the Order of the Garter.[55] He is betrothed to the Princess;[56] they are married in February 1613, with grand festivities and entertainments.[57] They depart in April, and sail away in the beautiful ship which had been built for Prince Henry.[58]

Reading through this volume, one can play the game of choosing the date at which Shakespeare wrote *Cymbeline*, and the date at which he revised it.

If this historical approach to *Cymbeline* is confirmed, it will mean that this Last Play belongs to the movement of Elizabethan revival in connection with Prince Henry and his sister, a movement with which James was only half-heartedly in favour, and which, after Henry's death, he abandoned for a policy of neutrality with Spain, abandoning also Princess Elizabeth and her husband who eventually ran into the total disaster of the Bohemian enterprise and the Thirty Years' War. Prince Henry's policies were perhaps dangerous; James's neutrality with Spain has been thought by many historians a wise course. The new interpretation of *Cymbeline* would seem to indicate that Shakespeare was a whole-hearted supporter of Prince Henry, and of Princess Elizabeth, the phoenix of a new Elizabethan age, leaders of the younger generation.

The Last Plays must be taken together, as a whole. We shall next attempt to explore the play of *Henry VIII*, the play in which Shakespeare expresses the Last Play themes in terms of real historical personages. We shall try to understand how the themes expressed in romance terms in *Cymbeline* are parallel to those expressed in terms of the Tudor Reformation in *Henry VIII*. The approach to *Henry VIII* will, it is hoped, support and corroborate the interpretation of *Cymbeline*.

Notes

1 Geoffrey of Monmouth, *The History of the Kings of Britain*, trans. Lewis Thorpe, Penguin Books, 1966, p. 119; cf. *Cymbeline*, ed. J. M. Nosworthy, Arden edition paperback, 1955, Introduction, pp. xvii–xviii.

2 *Faerie Queene*, II, x, 50–1.

3 *Astraea*, pp. 3 ff.

4 Ibid., pp. 29 ff.

5 G. Wilson Knight, *The Imperial Theme*, Oxford University Press, 1931; paperback, 1965.

6 *Astraea*, pp. 69 ff.

7 *Cymbeline*, V, iv, 138–45.

8 Ibid., V, v, 444–59.

9 Ibid., 467–8.

10 Ibid., 475–7.

11 Ibid., 479–86.

12 Emrys Jones, 'Stuart Cymbeline', *Essays in Criticism*, II, 1961, reprinted in *Shakespeare's Later Comedies*, ed. D. J. Palmer, pp. 248–62.

13 Bernard Harris, '*Cymbeline and Henry VIII*', *Later Shakespeare*, Stratford-upon-Avon Studies, 8, 1966, ed. J. R. Brown and B. Harris, pp. 203–33.

14 In his summary of the plot of *Cymbeline*, printed in E. K. Chambers, *William Shakespeare*, London, 1930, II, p. 339; and in *Cymbeline*, ed. J. M. Nosworthy, Introduction, p. iv.

15 Geoffrey of Monmouth, ed. cit., pp. 63, 75. Geoffrey spells the name 'Ignoge'.

16 In Spenser's version, Brut has three sons, 'Borne of faire Inogene of Italy', *Faerie Queene*, II, x, 13.

17 See above, p. 27.

18 Geoffrey of Monmouth, ed. cit., p. 55.

19 *Cymbeline*, V, iv, 30–113. In Geoffrey's story, Brut has a prophetic vision when asleep (ed. cit., p. 65).

20 See above, pp. 28–9.

21 See above, pp. 27–8.

22 *Polyolbion*, in *Works*, IV., ed. J. W. Hebel and K. Tillotson, Oxford University Press, 1961, p. 11.

23 Ibid., loc. cit.

24 For a pictorial representation of the Palatinate Lion associating with the British Lion, see *RE*, Pl. 8.

25 Thomas Campion, *The Lords' Masque*; see *RE*, p. 5; Stephen Orgel and Roy Strong, *Inigo Jones*, Sotheby, London, 1973, I, pp. 241–52.

26 *The Tempest*, ed. F. Kermode, Arden edition paperback, 1964, Introduction, p. xx; see below, pp. 92–3.

27 William Drummond of Hawthornden, 'Teares on the Death of Moeliades' (Elegy on the death of Prince Henry, 1613), in *Poems*, ed. W. C. Ward, The Muses' Library, n.d., I, pp. 1–12.

28 See *Cymbeline*, ed. J. M. Nosworthy, Introduction, pp. xxxvii–xl; *Philaster*, ed. A. Gurr, Introduction, pp. xxvii–xxviii, xlv–l.

29 Chambers, *The Elizabethan Stage*, London, 1923, IV, p. 180. As Gurr remarks (*Philaster*, Introduction, p. lxxii), 'The double entry may have been a clerical error . . . but Chambers accepts that it was performed twice against once for the other plays.'
30 G. Wilson Knight, *The Crown of Life*, Oxford University Press, 1947; paperback, 1965, p. 148.
31 *Cymbeline*, II, iv, 88.
32 Ibid., I, vii, 17.
33 John Donne, *Poems*, ed. H. J. C. Grierson, Oxford, 1912, I, pp. 127–31; quoted in modernised spelling as in Donne, *Poems*, ed. E. K. Chambers, The Muses' Library, I, p. 83.
34 *Cymbeline*, ed. J. M. Nosworthy, Introduction, p. lxxiii; Wilson Knight, *Crown of Life*, pp. 197, 200.
35 *Calendar of State Papers, Venice, Vol. XII, 1610–1631*, p. 31.
36 Ibid., p. 74.
37 Ibid., p. 106.
38 Ibid., p. 154.
39 Ibid., p. 194.
40 Ibid., p. 211.
41 Ibid., p. 278.
42 Ibid., p. 292.
43 Ibid., pp. 348–9.
44 Ibid., p. 365.
45 Ibid., p. 419.
46 Ibid., p. 402.
47 Ibid., p. 419.
48 Ibid., p. 439.
49 Ibid., p. 443.
50 Ibid., p. 446.
51 Ibid., p. 447.
52 Ibid., p. 448.
53 Ibid., p. 449.
54 Ibid., p. 450.
55 Ibid., p. 478.
56 Ibid., p. 476.
57 Ibid., pp. 498 ff.
58 Ibid., p. 523.

3

Henry VIII

Henry VIII is Shakespeare's last history play, the last of the sequence on the kings of England which began with *King John* (that is to say, King John was the earliest English king treated, whatever the date of the play may be). *Henry VIII* concludes the series, bringing it right up to recent times, for Queen Elizabeth I appears in it as an infant and James is alluded to as her successor at the end. And the play comes right up to the new generation, to the young people who are the hope of the future, for R. A. Foakes has pointed out in his introduction in the New Arden edition that the pageantry in the play is an allusion to the pageantry for the wedding of the Princess Elizabeth and the Elector Palatine.[1] Probably written and performed soon after that wedding, it was still being performed at the Globe a few months later, when the crackers let off to mark the entry of Henry VIII to Wolsey's masque set fire to the theatre. The following is the well-known contemporary description of the fire at the Globe:[2]

> The King's players had a new play, called *All is True*,
> representing some principal pieces of the reign of
> Henry VIII, which was set forth with many extraordinary
> circumstances of pomp and majesty, even to the matting
> of the stage; the Knights of the Order with their Georges

and garters, the Guards with their embroidered coats, and the like: sufficient in truth within a while to make greatness very familiar, if not ridiculous. Now, King Henry making a masque at the Cardinal Wolsey's house, and certain chambers being shot off at his entry, some of the paper, or other stuff, wherewith one of them was stopped, did light on the thatch, where being thought at first but an idle smoke, and their eyes more attentive to the show, it kindled inwardly, and ran round like a train, consuming within less than an hour the whole house to the very ground.

It seems certain that what fired the Globe was the stage direction in *Henry VIII* (I, iv, 49) 'chambers discharged' which marks the arrival of the king at Wolsey's banquet.

Since *Henry VIII* is described as a 'new play' around 29 June, 1613, the date of the burning of the Globe, and if there are allusions in it to the wedding of Princess Elizabeth and the Elector Palatine, which took place on 14 February, 1613, the play was presumably written and produced at some time between those dates. When the Globe was burned down during the production of a play which recalled the pageantry for her wedding, Princess Elizabeth had already arrived at Heidelberg, capital of the Palatinate, which she entered in state on 7 June.[3]

As for other Last Plays, the only early text is that in the First Folio of 1623. Heminges and Condell included this play in their famous collection of works by their late fellow-actor, William Shakespeare. In spite of this certificate of authenticity there has been a long tradition of doubt concerning the authorship. The most recent scholarship tends to confirm that Heminges and Condell were right, that *Henry VIII* is indeed a genuinely Shakespearean play. Foakes accepts the whole of the play as by Shakespeare;[4] other editors accept it as partly by Shakespeare but partly by another hand, probably Fletcher.[5] What has helped to reinstate *Henry VIII* in the Shakespearean canon is the recognition of the fact that, although it may seem somewhat different

66

from Shakespeare's earlier English history plays, it is like his Last Plays in its mood of reconciliation and tolerance, its masque-like effects, its mystical insights. It completes the sequence of the English history plays, bringing this up to date, but it is conceived in the mood of the Last Plays. Shakespeare is looking at English history for the last time, and from the standpoint of his latest mood.

From the point of view from which I am approaching the play, it is not a matter of great importance whether the whole play is actually written by Shakespeare or whether part of it is written by Fletcher. If there were two hands in the play, the outlook of the writers must have been identical, and it is with the politico-religious outlook that I am concerned, not with questions of style. Fletcher's view on the Sidney revival was evidently very close to that of Shakespeare, as we have seen. As a collaborator, he would therefore have seen eye to eye with Shakespeare on the general approach to historical and contemporary problems in *Henry VIII*.[6] It may be urged, however, that the new interpretation of *Cymbeline* as a masque-like reflection of the marriage of the Princess Elizabeth with the Elector Palatine, tends to confirm the total authenticity of *Henry VIII*. The treatment of real figures from English history in *Henry VIII* is parallel to the treatment of figures from mythical ancient British history in *Cymbeline*. And both plays reflect some culmination, or hoped-for culmination, of these religious and historical themes in the wedding of the Princess Elizabeth.

The editor of *Henry VIII* in the New Arden series rightly insists that the role of Henry should not be played as a fat, Holbeinesque caricature, but in a manner emphasising the grave role of monarch in the cosmic and religious sense which Shakespeare assigns to him. He also draws attention to Shakespeare's use in this play of John Foxe's *Acts and Monuments*,[7] the book which sets out the Tudor theory of imperial reform, the justification for the reform of the Church by a monarch exercising his sacred imperial power.

Foxe's book, more popularly known as *Foxe's Book of Martyrs*, with its striking illustrations of Protestant martyrs burning in the reign of Catholic Mary, was very well known to the Elizabethan and Jacobean public since it was placed in many churches for all to read. Its illustrations tell the story, not only of martyrs burning under Mary, but of Foxe's view of history as the age-long persecution of Emperors by Popes. His pictures show Emperors being oppressed by Papal tyranny, until that tyranny was finally thrown off by Henry VIII and kept at bay by his daughter, Elizabeth. Foxe's book reflects, and propagates, the whole theory of the Tudor reform of the Church as an imperial reform, the use of the sacred imperial or monarchical power to authorise reform of corruptions in the Church.[8] He leads up to the Tudor imperial reform through the history of sacred empire, quoting Dante on this theme.[9] Dante had appealed to the Emperor of his time to reform the Church. It is not generally realised that Tudor theologians, Bishop Jewel as well as Foxe, appealed to Dante in support of the Tudor imperial reform, thus introducing very wide and vast vistas of Dantesque universal order, as opposed to universal chaos, into their presentation of the Tudor theology. And Foxe, after outlining the history of sacred imperial theory, tells the story of the kings of England in terms of papal power versus imperial or monarchical power, with right and justice always on the side of the latter. The story culminates in the throwing off of the papal power by the imperial majesty of Henry VIII, and the appearance of his daughter as the royal virgin of the imperial reform.

Among those who certainly knew Foxe's book and its arguments very well was Shakespeare. Direct quotations from Foxe have been traced in at least three plays, *King John*, *Henry VI Part II*, and, above all, *Henry VIII*.

Shakespeare had read in Foxe's book the story of the poisoning of King John by the monk of Swineshead. The editor of *King John* in the New Arden edition discusses Shakespeare's borrowing of this episode from Foxe.[10] The villain of the piece, both in Foxe and in Shakespeare, is the papal legate who is supposed to have arranged the crime. Shakespeare is profoundly concerned in this play with the theme of papal versus royal authority. In Act III, John defies Cardinal Pandulph, charging him to tell the Pope that royal supremacy will not admit the 'usurped authority' of the Pope.[11] To speak of the 'usurped power', or 'usurped authority', of the Pope was to put into the mouth of a medieval king the language used by Tudor theologians when justifying the break with Rome. The Tudor royal supremacy, or imperial authority, casts off the illegal or 'usurped' authority of the Bishop of Rome.

Shakespeare's King John is not, however, uniformly the medieval prophet of Tudor reformation. He fell into sin when he connived at the murder of Arthur, the innocent bearer of an ancient British imperial name, and, at the beginning of Act V, he is shown basely giving in to pressure and acknowledging that it is from the Pope that he holds his crown. The crown is the central object in the opening words of the scene between King John and the legate.[12]

> *King John.* Thus have I yielded up into your hand
> The circle of my glory. (*Giving the crown.*)
> *Pandulph.*   Take again (*Giving back the crown.*)
> From this my hand, as holding of the pope,
> Your sovereign greatness and authority.

This scene would immediately relate, for an Elizabethan audience, to the propaganda which they saw all around them, the theme of the crown versus the papal tiara. The sacred royal and imperial crown, which should be held direct from God, is humiliated by indirect transmission through the Pope.

King John's base betrayal of the supremacy of the crown brings with it the woes threatened by Tudor historians and theologians of the school of Foxe. The papal legate 'blows up' the tempest of war, and England is invaded by foreign armies. Chaos takes the place of order. The 'infection of the time' brings forth 'injustice and confused wrong'.[13] And the legate instigates the crime of poisoning the king. The play goes down in murder, war, and misery. Written probably about 1590, in the years after the Armada, the play is a warning for the present, a reminder of how to ward off foreign invasion, war, and chaos by remaining true to the support of order and justice, the sacred royal power.

King John is an early play and John is the earliest of the historical kings of England whose history Shakespeare was to celebrate in the brilliant sequence of the English historical plays. It is therefore important to notice that Shakespeare's view of English history is, from the start, rooted in Foxe. Not only are there actual verbal quotations and parallels from Foxe in *King John* but the play (though of course it has other historical sources besides Foxe) reflects the Foxian apocalyptic view of English history as a conflict between the royal-imperial power and the papal power, with justice, order and peace on the side of the former, injustice and war on the side of the latter. This was precisely the lesson taught on all sides in the Tudor propaganda, that the Tudor imperial reform had brought peace and justice, whilst the Papacy was a stirrer up of war and disturbance and the enemy of the sacred imperial justice and peace.[14]

In Foxian history, the reigns of emperors, of distant mythical rulers, and of actual historical kings of England, are all preparations for the coming of the Tudor *renovatio*, the return of the ancient British race to rule, and the establishment of pure religion and virtue, peace and justice, by the Tudor imperial reform.[15] In the apocalyptic atmosphere of Tudor sacred imperialism, the Shakespearean presentation of royalty in terms of vast and age-long conflicts between good and evil, of cosmic harmony and music, or cosmic tempests and despair, would have had a resonance, or (to use a fashionable word) a relevance which can only be reconstructed historically by approaching Shakespeare through the history of the imperial theme.

I pass over quickly the sequence of the later English history plays in which it is not difficult to perceive the continued working out of the sacred imperial theme in relation to the characters and destinies of English kings. The themes of order and disorder are strong in *Henry IV*. A rebellious prelate summons up insurrection in the name of religion. A rebellious noble calls on the powers of chaos and paints a terrifying picture of universal anarchy breaking out at a time when the crown is not strong enough to maintain order. But when Henry IV is dying, his son, about to ascend the throne as Henry V, takes the crown from his pillow and tries it on. It is again one of the 'crown' scenes, in which the crown, here called an imperial crown,[16] is the centre of significance, about to pass to the monarch in whom, as presented by Shakespeare, the divine power of monarchy blazes out in all its strength. Having discarded his youthful vices, Henry V stands forth as representative of all the imperial virtues; he formally establishes Justice, though not forgetful of Clemency.[17] The Elizabethan audience, as they listened, would recall the all-pervasive imperialist propaganda of the age, with its presentation of the Monarch as possessed of Justice, Clemency, and all the imperial virtues.[18]

Finally, in *Henry VIII*, we have the culmination of Foxian history with the throwing off of the papal power in the name of the sacred majesty of the Monarch. There are definite quotations from Foxe in this play, as already mentioned, and Henry is presented in all seriousness as representing kingship in its religious and reforming role. To quote the words of the editor of the play in the Arden series:[19]

> If God alone is stable, he has a high priest on
> earth, in the person of Henry. . . . He is usually played
> as bluff King Hal, costumed and paunched as grossly
> as in the late portraits, with a full swagger, and a
> nervous eagerness to cry 'Ha!' The playwright's
> conception surely embodies more than such a portrait,
> which enlarges incidentals, like the King's
> peremptoriness, into his whole character. All that
> can be said of his physical appearance is that he is
> lusty and vigorous, and the dramatic impression is of
> youth. Much more important than his physical
> characteristics is his growth in spiritual stature

during the play. Henry is shown as a strong, regal
figure, the embodiment of authority; but initially
this authority is obscured under the sway of Wolsey.
Henry's progress in the play is to throw off the
domination of Wolsey. . . . As long as Wolsey's sway
persists, injustice is done, to Buckingham and
to Katharine, for whose downfall the Cardinal is
presented as mainly responsible. At the fall of Wolsey,
Henry emerges in the full panoply of kingship; from
this point all goes well and Cranmer is saved through
[the King's] direct intervention in council. When
he administers the law himself, justice as of heaven
operates, and in his assumption of control Henry may
be compared to Prospero, for he seems to stand
above fate.

This interpretation of the scenes of Henry's rejection of Wolsey,
his support of Cranmer, shows us Henry as the monarch of the
Tudor imperial reform, purifying the Church with the sword of
royal justice. The grouping of the characters in these scenes
recalls one of the most notable illustrations in Foxe's book, the
picture which shows Henry seated on the throne of royal
majesty, dismissing the papal representatives and honouring
Cranmer, who holds the open Bible.[20] Exactly so in *Henry VIII*
does Henry cast down Wolsey to his fall whilst raising Cranmer,
in a scene in which the King reaches a full stature of majesty,
a majesty of kingship freed from papal interference, exercising
imperial reforming powers.

In *Henry VIII*, Wolsey represents 'Popery' as understood by
the Reformers; he amasses money and is avaricious, intending to
use this money drawn by unjust extortion out of the country
to purchase offices. He is presented as self-indulgent and lecherous, proud and arrogant; he embodies pride, avarice, impurity,
those vices of a corrupt Church against which the imperialist
reformers, including Dante, had always inveighed.[21] These
contrasting vices were always implicit in the symbolism used of

the virtues of Queen Elizabeth I, the Just Virgin of the imperial reform, the 'Astraea' who returns in a golpen age of pure religion. The virtues of the Tudor imperial reform are emphasised once again in this last history play, and Shakespeare openly recalls in it their full expression in Queen Elizabeth I. Just as Foxe led up to Queen Elizabeth as the culmination of his history, so does the infant Elizabeth, borne to her christening, appear in *Henry VIII*, and Cranmer prophesies for her a glorious destiny.

Yet, though it restates the basic themes of the imperial reform, there is in this play a gentle atmosphere of tolerance for all the actors in that great drama of the past, whether Catholic or Protestant. Katharine of Aragon is most sympathetically treated as a good woman, suffering undeservedly. With amazing tact, this recognition of the virtues of Katharine is combined with affection for Anne Boleyn, admired for her beauty and youth and respected for her religion which is clearly indicated as Lutheran. 'I know her for a spleeny Lutheran', says Wolsey of Anne. Yet in the tolerant atmosphere of a Last Play, good people are admired for their goodness and their religious sincerity, whatever their actual religious affiliation may be. Katharine, who often refers to her Spanish-Catholic relatives, is deeply respected. Cranmer, the Protestant, or 'sectary' as Wolsey calls him, is an honest and sincere man and recognised as such, in contrast to Wolsey, by the King. Even Wolsey, though as the representative of the pride, avarice, and luxury of the Whore of Babylon he must fall before the reforming Monarch, is treated with sympathy in his misfortunes. And the infant Elizabeth, seen on her first progress, returning from her christening amid admiring crowds, inspires Cranmer to give prophetic utterance. This royal infant, now in her cradle, promises a thousand blessings on this land. She will be a pattern to all princes, attended by all virtues.[22]

> In her days every man shall eat in safety
> Under his own vine what he plants, and sing
> The merry songs of peace to all his neighbours.
> God shall be truly known. . . .

Thus in the year 1613, ten years after the death of the great Queen, Shakespeare is joining in a revival of the Elizabethan traditions and of the Elizabeth cult.

And Shakespeare is remembering and reviving the symbols of the Elizabeth cult, particularly the phoenix. From his paean on the Elizabethan *pax*, Cranmer passes on to prophesy the rebirth of the phoenix, the rebirth of the Elizabeth tradition in her successor.[23]

> Nor shall this peace sleep with her; but, as when
> The bird of wonder dies, the maiden phoenix
> Her ashes new create another heir
> As great in admiration as herself,
> So shall she leave her blessedness to one . . .
> Who from the sacred ashes of her honour
> Shall star-like rise. . . .

This phoenix is James, but the allusion includes his children, through the image of the cedar and its branches:[24]

> He shall flourish
> And like a mountain cedar, reach his branches
> To all the plains about him. . . .

This was the image through which James and his children were described at the end of *Cymbeline*.[25] Though the main branch, Prince Henry, was gone when *Henry VIII* was written, the other branch, Princess Elizabeth, had recently been the centre of the brilliant pageantry of her wedding.

In his introduction to *Henry VIII* in the Arden edition, R. A. Foakes suggests that the great Protestant wedding was an auspicious moment for the writing by Shakespeare of a last history play glorifying the Tudor reformation. He thinks that the splendid processions in the play, on the occasions of Anne Boleyn's wedding, and the christening of her infant daughter, reflect the glorious progress of Princess Elizabeth to the bridal ceremony,[26] and that the masques at Wolsey's house, and other events in the play, would recall the amazing series of masques and celebrations in honour of the recent wedding.[27]

> In particular, the climax to which the play leads,
> the birth of the princess who was to become Queen
> Elizabeth I, affords a link with this event [with the
> wedding of Princess Elizabeth]. For many, the
> occasion revived memories of the palmy days of the
> great Queen; Princess Elizabeth was following her
> namesake in her support of the true religion if not
> in getting married, and a comparison or identification
> of the two is common.

Foakes then gives examples of comparisons of Princess Elizabeth with Queen Elizabeth I, and of the use of Elizabeth symbolism of the Princess. He emphasises that Princess Elizabeth was seen as a phoenix,[28] a rebirth of the great Queen, and remarks that the phoenix passage in Cranmer's speech would remind the audience of Princess Elizabeth as the new phoenix. He has arrived at a similar core of interpretation as was arrived at in my interpretation of *Cymbeline*, in which the imagery of that play is seen as related to the Elizabethan revival, and particularly to the revival of Elizabeth symbols around Princess Elizabeth. Foakes's interpretation of *Henry VIII* and my interpretation of *Cymbeline* would thus seem to match one another. Both plays belong to the Elizabethan revival at the time of Princess Elizabeth's wedding, and both use the imagery of that revival. I suggest that the new interpretation of *Cymbeline* tends to confirm the full Shakespearean authorship of *Henry VIII*. Two plays so close in mood, in historical outlook, and in imagery, are surely likely to be by the same author.

Foakes notes that the image of the cedar spreading its branches had been used of Princess Elizabeth in sermons, prophesying the advent of children born of her.[29] He does not note a significant point about the cedar image, that it connects with *Cymbeline*, and with the presentation in that play of James as the cedar, with his children as branches. In *Cymbeline* the royal cedar had several branches; since then, one has been lopped off in the death of Prince Henry. All hopes for the future now centre on Princess Elizabeth and on her marriage.

The two plays belong to the hour in which King James seemed whole-heartedly on the side of the Union of Protestant Princes, to the head of which he was marrying his daughter. They seize the moment in which James seemed identified with the Elizabethan revival, with which he was not really in sympathy as was soon to appear. At the time of the wedding the future disasters were not foreseen. All seemed joy and hope, and that the people of the younger generation would repair the mistakes of their elders. The linking of *Cymbeline* with *Henry VIII*, which is now possible through new understanding of the reference of *Cymbeline* to contemporary history, may eventually be seen as a new key with which to unlock many Shakespearean problems.

For *Henry VIII* is a Last Play in which the contemporary references of Last Plays are made explicit. In it we have the theme of the long expanse of time, covering generations, and allowing for the arrival of new generations who will heal and resolve the discords of old times. And here the new generations are historical personages. Queen Elizabeth I arrives in it as a child to renew the times after the preceding convulsions. And yet newer generations are coming through Princess Elizabeth's wedding and its promise. The new generations, alluded to in myths and romances in the romantic plays, are given concrete historical expression in the history play.

Above all, the history play makes clear what were the discords and sadnesses of old times with which the new generations will do away. They are the discords in religion, the 'jars' between Catholics and Protestants which Prince Henry thought that he knew a way of removing, and which the tolerance and kindliness of Shakespeare to both sides in *Henry VIII* seems to indicate. In the play, this new tolerance and kindliness seems connected with new visions, new revelations of the divine, the 'theophanies' which are typical of Last Plays and of which there are several examples in the last history play.

One of these moments of insight comes during the singing of the magical song to the sad Katharine as she sits with her women at work:

> Orpheus with his lute made trees
> And the mountain tops that freeze,
>   Bow themselves when he did sing.

The atmosphere of this marvellous song lifts the play for a moment out of the cruel world of religious controversy on to another level, opened up by the magical union of poetry and music.[30]

> In sweet music is such art,
> Killing care and grief of heart
>   Fall asleep, or hearing die.

These are the strains of universal harmony heard above the discords of life. And one is reminded by this song, and its effects on the hearers, of Marsilio Ficino's revival of what he believed to be ancient. Orphic singing,[31] which was practised in France in Baïf's Academy of Poetry and Music.[32] Shakespeare had certainly heard of that Academy for he refers to it in *Love's Labour's Lost*.[33] In Baïf's Academy, Catholic and Protestant musicians practised together their measured poetry and music, with the deliberate aim of soothing the terrible discords of the French wars of religion through the 'effects' of music. The Orphic singing in *Henry VIII* might have had a similar purpose.

To Katharine is allotted another moment of vision. She sees in her sleep a band of spirits bearing garlands of bay who trip over the stage in masque-like fashion and are seen by the audience but not by Katharine's companions. The vision brings into the history play a suggestion of the masque, of the masque-like effects common to all Last Plays. Katharine's words describe the vision:[34]

> Saw you not even now a blessed troop
> Invite me to a banquet, whose bright faces

Cast thousand beams upon me, like the sun?
They promis'd me eternal happiness. . . .

The good dying Catholic sees the heavenly vision. And the good Protestant, Cranmer, is seized with the spirit of prophecy. It would seem that, beyond all earthly jars, Shakespeare envisaged a union of the good.

It is now possible to compare Shakespeare's mode of referring to a contemporary theme in a history play and in a romance play. In *Cymbeline* and *Henry VIII*, Shakespeare is using the two types of history, the mythical, romantic, 'British' type of history, and straight history of real historical monarchs of England. Through the Tudor myth of British descent he can use a mythical British-History character, Cymbeline, and a real Tudor king, Henry VIII, to make his contemporary points about his hopes for the youngest royal generation. The play on real history shares with the romance the atmosphere of the Last Plays, in which new theophanies, new visions of the divine, are experienced in an atmosphere of reconciliation. The theophanies in *Henry VIII* reveal mystical experience in which the religious discords of the past are reconciled. The vision in *Cymbeline*, and its interpretation by the soothsayer, express a mystical view of expanded religious-imperial destiny. The return to mythical Romano-British imperialism in *Cymbeline* matches the return to Tudor Protestant imperialism in *Henry VIII*.

The comparison of the two plays, as now understood, gives an insight into the Elizabeth outlook, which is being deliberately revived. It shows us how Elizabethan Protestantism and its imagery of purity and chastity implying a pure reformed religion, was inextricably blended with the Elizabethan chivalric idea. The purity of Arthur and his knights, or Protestant chivalric ethics, combines with the theological purity of the reformed religion to form the imagery surrounding the Virgin Queen in the Elizabethan age,[35] and which Shakespeare is still using of Princess Elizabeth in the Jacobean age. It is this double historical line of the ancient purity of British chivalric tradition, combined with

the theological purity of royal and Tudor reformation, which
informs this poetic view of history. The Reformation line informs
it politically, and justifies the break with Rome, the British line
joins this with chivalric tradition, with knightly purity, and
opens the door to mysticism, myth, and magic.

There is in this outlook something closely akin to the Renaissance belief in *prisca theologia*, in the purity and religious value
of traditions stemming from supposed ancient sages,[36] from
Hermes Trismegistus, the supposed Egyptian soothsayer and
teacher of Hermetic philosophy and magic, or from Zoroaster,
or from Orpheus, or other teachers of supposedly ancient truth,
in whom the Renaissance Neoplatonist found a justification for
his belief in a synthesis of all religious truth on a level of mystical
insight and magical intuition. It is the blend of pure British
prisca theologia and Tudor reform with all the wealth of Renaissance Neoplatonism and its magical core, with the unlimited
richness of imagery which this opened up, which informs
Spenser's Elizabethan epic. Centred on the Virgin Queen,
Spenser's poem combines British and Tudor history as the base
for the deployment of his argument.[37] So, too, does Sidney use
British and chivalric reformation as the base for Arcadian
romance infused with Renaissance influences.

I would see the Last Plays as a whole as an archaising revival,
a deliberate return to the past by an old Elizabethan living in the
Jacobean age. There is the basic return to Tudor theology, to
the emphasis on the imperial reform of the Church, and all that
that implied. There is a return to the Elizabethan chivalric ideal,
perhaps first visible in *Pericles* in which a knight seems to return
from the sea of death to take part in an Elizabethan Accession
Day Tilt.[38] There is the pervasive influence of Sidney's *Arcadia*
in all the Last Plays, indicating a return to the Sidney legend
and its cultivation in Arcadian romance. We return in the Last
Plays, or so I suggest, to the world of Shakespeare's youth and
its ideals, ideals which he had somehow lost in the terrible
period of the great tragedies but which he now hopes to see
reviving in the younger generation. And the past is not revived

in a merely antiquarian manner. It revives because there is a
new outpouring of the deep influences which had vivified it,
new visions which correct the narrowness of the past, and give
hope of wider solutions now possible, in the present or in
the future.

Hitherto, the attempts to relate Shakespeare to the history
of his times have concentrated mainly on the Elizabethan Shakespeare. Shakespeare and the Jacobean age is a less familiar topic
than Shakespeare and the Elizabethan age. This comparative
neglect of the historical climate of Shakespeare's later years
corresponds to the general neglect, in the history of Europe
as a whole, of the early years of the seventeenth century. History
falls inexorably into 'periods': for Europe as a whole it divides
into the Renaissance and the seventeenth century; for England,
it divides into the Elizabethan age and the Stuart age. In this
periodisation, the important interstices tend to be overlooked,
the times between the periods, times when survivors from an
earlier period are still alive and influential, times when an earlier
period has not fully ceased and the new period is not yet fully
born. The first fifteen or so years of the seventeenth century
were such a time in all Europe, a time when the Renaissance
was not yet fully ended, though its end was in sight, and survivors of the older liberalism dreaded the new tyrannies spreading
over Europe and the coming final disaster in the renewed outbreak of the wars of religion in the Thirty Years' War.

In that anxious time, James I of Great Britain had a tremendous
reputation in Europe. He was believed to represent the Elizabethan tradition of opposition to Spanish-Hapsburg ambition
and to the more repressive aspects of Counter Reformation. Not
only Protestant Europe looked towards James as a beacon of
hope, but also liberal Catholics. He seemed to support Paolo
Sarpi and the Venetian stand against papal aggression.[39] He
seemed to be working in unison with Henri IV of France. His
much advertised profound theological learning was believed to
include – and did in fact include – plans for religious reunion,
or for religious toleration,[40] such as had inspired liberal theo-

logians in the sixteenth century. Such hopes were far from dead
in the early seventeenth century, and who was more suited to
bring them to fruition than the British Solomon? In the first
nine or so years of his reign, James appeared to be living up
to this reputation. During these years he appeared to be moving
towards the support of those opposed to the Spanish-Hapsburg
powers. The culminating point of James's European reputation
was the moment when he married his daughter to the German
leader of the opposition.[41]

Afterwards he shifted away from that position, tending more
and more towards placating Spain and deeply involving himself
in the long drawn out agony of the proposed Spanish match for
his son, Charles (Prince of Wales after the death of Henry).
Proposed Spanish matches were the constantly recurring problem
of the reign of James; they typified his aim of peace through
appeasement. After the death of Henry and the departure of
Elizabeth – the children who represented the hopes raised by
the earlier James – the King retreated from the Elizabethan
revival and towards the supine cultivation of the enemies
who despised him. His supreme betrayal of the Elizabethan
tradition was his execution of Walter Raleigh at the behest of
Spain.

Perhaps the true reading of events was that of the Venetian
observer who thought that it was Prince Henry who stiffened
his father's resolution and that it was after the death of the
Prince that James gave way to his nervous terrors.[42] John Donne
may also be implying this when he says in his elegy on Prince
Henry that the Prince[43]

> Was his great father's greatest instrument,
> And activest spirit, to convey and tie
> This soul of peace through Christianity?
> Was it not well believed, that he would make
> This general peace th' eternal overtake,
> And that his times might have stretched out so far
> As to touch those of which they emblems are?

Donne's obscure excitement conveys the feeling of what the loss of Prince Henry meant.

It is to the period of the Elizabethan Renaissance within the Jacobean age that I would refer Shakespeare's plays of *Cymbeline*, with its revival of the Tudor British-imperial theme, and of *Henry VIII* with its revival of the Tudor imperial reform. It seems to me that these plays provide a possibility of drawing nearer to Shakespeare's attitudes to events and movements of his own times than perhaps any of his other works. The approach to them attempted here demands, however, more detailed study before it can become a firm basis for exploration of Shakespearean problems as a whole.

I shall now attempt the study of the deeper thought influences informing the Last Plays, which may also appear as, in part, an Elizabethan revival or return to the past, though there seem to have been new sources for such influences available. And here also, in the exploration of this deepest line, we shall find ourselves involved with the younger royal generation and the movements around it.

Notes

1 *Henry VIII*, ed. R. A. Foakes, Arden edition paperback, 1958, Introduction, pp. xxx–xxxv.
2 The source of this constantly quoted account is in Henry Wotton, *Reliquae Wottonianae* (1671 edition, pp. 425–6).
3 *RE*, pp. 9–11.
4 *Henry VIII*, ed. R. A. Foakes, Introduction, pp. xv–xxviii.
5 *Henry VIII*, ed. J. C. Maxwell, Cambridge University Press, 1962, Introduction.
6 The Shakespeare-Fletcher collaboration in *The Two Noble Kinsmen* strongly indicates an approach to contemporary problems very close to that of Shakespeare in *Cymbeline*.
7 *Henry VIII*, ed. R. A. Foakes, Introduction, pp. xxxv–xxxix. The story of Cranmer in Act V is based on Foxe's book, which also provided hints for the treatment of Wolsey in the last three acts. 'Some speeches are little more than Holinshed or Foxe versified' (ibid., p. xxxviii).

8   For Foxe as a source for the concept of the imperial reform of the Church
    in relation to the Tudors, see *Astraea*, pp. 42–7. The illustrations in
    Foxe's book, which clarify his argument, are reproduced in *Astraea*,
    Pls. 4, 5.
9   *Astraea*, pp. 45–7.
10 *King John*, ed. E. A. J. Honigmann, Arden edition, 1954, paperback, 1967,
    Introduction, p. xiv. Cf. *Astraea*, p. 44.
11 *King John*, III, i, 86.
12 Ibid., V, i, 1–4.
13 Ibid., V, ii, 20–3.
14 *Astraea*, pp. 38 ff. The presentation of the Papacy as an instigator of
    war against peaceful Emperors was a legacy from the medieval sacred
    imperial tradition; see *Astraea*, pp. 8 ff.
15 *Astraea*, pp. 42 ff.
16 *Henry IV, Part II*, IV, v, 41.
17 *Henry V*, II, ii, 2.
18 *Astraea*, pp. 59 ff.
19 *Henry VIII*, ed. R. A. Foakes, Introduction, pp. lxi–lxii.
20 *Astraea*, Pl. 5a.
21 *Astraea*, pp. 24–5, 122, etc.
22 *Henry VIII*, V, v, 33–6.
23 Ibid., 39–44.
24 Ibid., 52–4.
25 *Cymbeline*, V, v, 454–9.
26 *Henry VIII*, ed. R. A. Foakes, Introduction, pp. xxx–xxxv.
27 Ibid., p. xxxii.
28 Cf. John Donne on this theme, quoted above, p. 56.
29 Foakes, Introduction, p. xxxviii. The image is, of course, Biblical in
    origin. See also Bernard Harris, '*Cymbeline* and *Henry VIII*', *Later Shakespeare*,
    New York, 1967, p. 232.
30 *Henry VIII*, III, i, 3–5.
31 D. P. Walker, *Spiritual and Demonic Magic from Ficino to Campanella*,
    Warburg Institute, 1947 (Kraus Reprint, 1967), pp. 22–4.
32 *Academies*, pp. 70–6; *Tapestries*, pp. 86–8; *Bruno*, pp. 175–6; *Astraea*,
    pp. 138–40, 151–65
33 *Academies*, pp. 264–5; *Bruno*, pp. 356–7; *Astraea*, pp. 211–12.
34 *Henry VIII*, IV, ii, 87–90.
35 *Astraea*, pp. 122 ff.
36 D. P. Walker, *The Ancient Theology*, Duckworth, London, 1972, pp. 63–
    131.
37 *Astraea*, pp. 69 ff.
38 On the Elizabethan Accession Day Tilts, see *Astraea*, pp. 88 ff. The
    scene in *Pericles*, II, ii, must surely be meant to recall such tilts. Though
    Shakespeare did not himself write this scene he must surely have approved
    of it and meant it to be incorporated with his part of the play.
39 See my article, 'Paolo Sarpi's *History of the Council of Trent*', *Journal of the
    Warburg and Courtauld Institutes*, VII (1944), pp. 123–43.

40 D. H. Willson, *King James VI and I*, London, 1956, paperback, 1963, pp. 219 ff.
41 *RE*, pp. 1–14.
42 *Calendar of State Papers, Venice, Vol. XII*, 1610–1631, p. 450.
43 'Elegy upon the untimely death of the incomparable Prince Henry', *Poems*, ed. H. J. C. Grierson, Oxford, 1912, I, pp. 265–70; ed. E. K. Chambers, The Muses' Library, II, p. 72.

4

Magic in the Last Plays:
The Tempest

To treat of magic, or the magical atmosphere, in Shakespeare one ought to include all the plays, for such an atmosphere is certainly present in his earlier periods. In the Last Plays this atmosphere becomes very strong indeed and, moreover, it becomes more clearly associated with the great traditions of Renaissance magic – magic as an intellectual system of the universe, foreshadowing science, magic as a moral and reforming movement, magic as the instrument for uniting opposing religious opinions in a general movement of Hermetic reform. All these aspects were present in Giordano Bruno's missionary enterprises, in his new system of the universe, in his Hermetic religion of love and magic which he preached throughout Europe, and particularly in England from 1582 to 1585,[1] Shakespeare's formative years. The influence of Bruno is, I believe, to be felt in *Love's Labour's Lost*[2] in which four members of a 'French Academy' (Bruno came to England with a politico-religious message from the French King) are drawn together, probably echoing the efforts of Baïf's Academy of Poetry and Music to draw together Catholics and Huguenots through the incantatory influences of poetry and music. Thus Shakespeare, or so I believe, knew of the larger religious aims of Renaissance magic even in his earlier plays. The late plays show fresh infusions of such influences, and I confine my discussion of this immense subject to 'Magic in the Last Plays'.

The first Last Play, the first to show the peculiarities of plot and atmosphere common to all Last Plays, would appear to have been *Pericles*, though caution must be used in speaking of this play about which so much is uncertain. Amongst the uncertainties is its date of composition, though we know that it cannot be later than 1608 when the first printed edition was entered in the Stationers' Register.[3] *Pericles* differs from other Last Plays in its textual history, since it was several times printed from 1609 onwards, whilst all the other Last Plays were first printed in the First Folio of 1623. In spite of the peculiarities of this play, and the fact that not all of it is by Shakespeare, it is now generally accepted as a Last Play. And in this play, Shakespeare introduces a great magus figure in the character of Cerimon. Though he took the name, Cerimon, and the fact that he is a doctor, from his source, Gower's *Confessio Amantis*,[4] the Cerimon of *Pericles* is a highly significant new creation.

After the great storm, and in contrast to it, we are introduced into the peaceful atmosphere of Cerimon's house. The doctor has, he tells us, ever 'studied physic', and learned the secret properties of metals, stones, plants, holding that knowledge and virtue may make 'a man a god'.[5] We hear of his charity, how he has healed hundreds, and given of his own wealth to relieve poverty. To this Good Physician, the sailors bring the chest which has been tossed up on the shore by the storm. It is opened and reveals Thaissa, apparently a lifeless corpse. But Cerimon perceives that there may still be life in her, orders fires to be lighted, and prepares medicaments. He applies warmth, and commands music to sound. Presently Thaissa begins to move and to 'blow into life's flower again'.[6]

We have seen a skilled physician at work, and more than a physician, for divinely healing influences flow from Cerimon. He is an almost Christ-like figure who goes about healing the sick, not for payment, but out of his pure benevolence and charity. We seem to sense here an influence of the new ideal of the physician spreading in Europe through the influence of Paracelsus, in whom new medical skills are combined with a reputation for new magic. Cerimon uses 'musical therapy' in his healing, and his power of bringing to life again seems a miracle to the beholders.

Does Cerimon remind us of the Rosicrucian Brothers, who, as described in the first Rosicrucian manifesto, the *Fama*, were an Order devoted to healing the sick *gratis*?[7] So far as we know, the earliest date at which the *Fama* may have been circulating is 1610,[8] and this play cannot be later than 1608. Nevertheless, the Rosicrucian manifestos undoubtedly reflect a movement which was in existence earlier. Be that as it may (and I am not attempting more than a suggestion here) it can be said that Cerimon has something of a Rosicrucian aura about him. He is the magus as physician, rather than the magus as physical scientist, like Prospero. He did not actually perform the miracle of raising the dead to life; Thaissa was not really dead. Yet Cerimon himself says that great knowledge and skill may 'make a man a god', and his appearance after the storm suggests an almost miraculous peace-bringing and healing power.

Another Last Play, *The Winter's Tale*, repeats the theme of the bringing to life of a woman apparently dead. And in the case of Paulina and the supposed statue of Hermione, Shakespeare makes what appears to me to be a most pointed and precise allusion to deep Hermetic magic.

Let us think again of that strange scene.[9] Hermione is believed by her husband to have died long ago. Paulina says that she has a statue of her which is a remarkable likeness. She shows this supposed statue to the King and the assembled court. 'O royal piece,' cries the King, 'there's magic in thy majesty.' Paulina claims that she can, if the King wills it, make the statue 'move indeed, descend, and take you by the hand'. But then, she adds, 'you'll think . . . I am assisted by wicked powers.' The King urges her to try her art. Paulina commands all to stand still, but those who think she is about unlawful business, let them depart. 'Proceed,' commands the King. 'No foot shall stir.' Thus authorised to do magic which some may think unlawful, Paulina orders music to sound, and adjures the supposed statue to descend. The statue comes to life, being, of course, really the living Hermione.

Thus Paulina did not really do magic in breathing life into a dead image, for the statue was a living woman (just as Cerimon's magical medical skill revived a woman who was not really dead). Nevertheless, Shakespeare undoubtedly alludes to magic in this scene, and, I believe, to a particular kind of magic.

As is now well known, the writings attributed to the supposed 'Hermes Trismegistus' had an immense influence in the Renaissance and were associated with Neoplatonism as the Hermetic core of that movement. Of the writings supposedly by Hermes Trismegistus, some teach a vaguely pious 'religion of the world' but some are overtly magical, particularly the *Asclepius*, the dialogue in which Hermes describes the religious magic through which the ancient Egyptian priests were supposed to infuse life into the statues of their gods, by various rites and practices, including musical accompaniment.[10] Many Renaissance admirers of Hermes as a religious philosopher excluded the *Asclepius* from the Hermetic canon because of disapproval of the magic.[11] But an all-out religious Hermetist, such as Giordano Bruno, includes the magic of the *Asclepius* as a basic part of his message, the announcement of a coming magical-religious reform in which the world will return to a lost better state. Bruno's preaching of this magical-religious mission, in his Italian dialogues published in England, is full of echoes of the god-making passage in the *Asclepius*, interpreted as a profound understanding of nature, and of the divine in nature.[12]

It seems obvious, though I do not think that this has ever been pointed out, that Shakespeare is alluding, in the scene of Paulina and the statue, to the famous god-making passage in the *Asclepius*. The audience is warned that something deeply magical is afoot which some may think unlawful. 'Proceed', commands the King. How does Shakespeare intend the allusion to be taken? Does he use the Hermetic life-infusing magic as a metaphor of the artistic process? Here we become involved in deep debate, which I leave on one side. Let us rest content, for the moment, with the probability that Shakespeare knew the god-making passage in the *Asclepius* and regarded it as in some way profoundly important. The bringing to life of Hermione is in fact the core of the message of the play, the return to life of a lost and banished goodness and virtue.

The return of Hermetic or 'Egyptian' magical religion involves, in the Hermetic texts and in Giordano Bruno's interpretation of them, the return of moral law, the banishment of vice, the renewal of all good things, a holy and most solemn restoration of nature herself.[13] There is perhaps something of this magical religious and moral philosophy in the profundities about 'nature' in *The Winter's Tale*. The episode of Paulina's daring magic, with its allusion to the magical statues of the *Asclepius*, may thus be a key to the meaning of the play as an expression of one of the deepest currents of Renaissance magical philosophy of nature.

We have touched on the mysterious aspects of *Cymbeline*, its moments of revelation interpreted by the soothsayer who bears the significant name of 'Philarmonus'. The central mystery of the cave in *Cymbeline* is only partly explained by reference to the scenes of Prince Henry's masques and the coming to life of the Lady Chivalry and the magician Merlin in a cave setting in those shows. There is some further hidden, or esoteric, meaning in the cave which makes one wonder whether Rosicrucian symbolism, or something like it, might already have been current before the actual publication of the Rosicrucian manifestos. The central symbol of the *Fama* is the vault or cave in which something long lost is found, the tomb of Christian Rosencreutz which was accidentally discovered in a vault (according to the fiction recounted in the *Fama*) and the opening of which was the signal for the revival of the Rosicrucian Order.[14] The revived chivalrous magic of *Cymbeline* leads in due course to a vast religious peace, an outpouring of new religious revelation in which all discord is harmonised.

When these themes are translated into actual history in *Henry VIII*, we have the solution of old religious quarrels in the sympathetic treatment of both Catholic and Protestant goodness. The magical atmosphere is present, represented particularly by the Orphic singing, perhaps reminiscent, as I have suggested, of those efforts towards religious reconciliation through the cultivation of incantatory singing, as practised in Baïf's Academy of Poetry and Music.

Finally we come to the Last Play which is the supreme expression of the magical philosophy of the Last Plays, The Tempest, the play which everyone knows.

First, let us consider the textual history of The Tempest.[15] Like all Last Plays, except Pericles and Henry VIII, it seems to have had a first appearance around 1610–11, or at least a play called The Tempest was performed at court in 1611. Unlike Cymbeline and The Winter's Tale it was apparently not seen by Simon Forman at about that time, so we do not have his plot summary to compare with the play as we have it. Like The Winter's Tale, it was one of the plays by Shakespeare which were performed by the King's Men before Princess Elizabeth and her betrothed in 1612. Like all Last Plays except Pericles it was first printed in the First Folio of 1623 where it is the first play in that famous volume.

Thus the history of The Tempest follows the familiar pattern and there is room for an earlier version of the play to have been revised to suit performance before Princess Elizabeth and the Palatine. This has in fact been suggested in critical discussions of the play, summed up by Frank Kermode in his introduction to the Arden edition, where it is pointed out that the masque in the play, which is evidently a nuptial masque, was perhaps added to an earlier version to make it suitable for performance before the princely pair.[16] Thus, The Tempest, as we have it, would enter that atmosphere of masque and pageantry surrounding the wedding of Princess Elizabeth which is central for the understanding of Cymbeline and which Foakes has detected in Henry VIII. I would further suggest that the emphasis on chastity before marriage in The Tempest, where it is so marked a feature of Prospero's advice to the young prince,[17] should be compared with the treatment of the same theme in *Philaster*,[18] the play by Beaumont and Fletcher performed before Elizabeth and the Palatine at the same time, in which the overtures made before marriage to his betrothed by the Spanish prince, seem to be a mark of the impurity of a Spanish match. Prospero is perhaps emphasising that his daughter is *not* making a Spanish match.

The themes of *The Tempest* connect with the Last Play themes as a whole. There is a young generation, Ferdinand and Miranda, the very young princely pair, and an older generation, Prospero and his contemporaries, divided by bitter wrongs and quarrels but brought together at the end in the magical atmosphere of reconciliation. *The Tempest* fits very well into our general historical approach to the Last Plays with its argument that these 'reconciliation through a younger generation' themes belong into an actual historical situation in which Prince Henry and his sister were seen as hopeful figures of this kind. Prince Henry being now dead, only a daughter and her lover represent the young generation in *The Tempest*. Miranda has no brother. Nor indeed have Perdita or Marina. Only Imogen has brothers, and *Cymbeline* was not performed after the death of Prince Henry and before Frederick and Elizabeth, as were *The Winter's Tale* and *The Tempest*.

We have now to think about magic in *The Tempest*. What kind of magic is it? This is a problem which has been considerably discussed in recent years and I am not bringing forward any very new or startling discovery in observing that Prospero, as a magus, appears to work on the lines indicated in that well-known textbook of Renaissance magic, the *De occulta philosophia* of Henry Cornelius Agrippa. Frank Kermode was a pioneer in pointing to Agrippa as a power behind Prospero's art in his introduction to *The Tempest* in the Arden edition, first published in 1954. Prospero as a magus, says Kermode, exercises a discipline of virtuous knowledge; his art is the achievement of 'an intellect pure and conjoined with the powers of the gods without which [and this is direct quotation by Kermode from Agrippa] we shall never happily ascend to the scrutiny of secret things, and to the power of wonderful workings'.[19] In short, Prospero has learned that 'occult philosophy' which Agrippa taught and knows how to put it into practice. Moreover, like Agrippa, Shakespeare makes very clear in *The Tempest* how utterly different is the high intellectual and virtuous magic of the true magus from low and filthy witchcraft and sorcery. Prospero is poles apart from the witch Sycorax and her evil son. Indeed, Prospero as the good magus has a reforming mission; he clears the world of his island from the evil magic of the witch; he rewards the good characters and punishes the wicked. He is a just judge, or a virtuous and reforming monarch, who uses his magico-scientific powers for good. The triumph of a liberal and Protestant Reformation in *Henry VIII* has its counterpart in *The Tempest* in the triumph of a reforming magus in the dream world of the magical island.

Prospero's magic is then a good magic, a reforming magic. But what exactly is the intellectual structure or system within which his magic works? Here we have to turn to Agrippa's definitions which can be simplified, rather drastically, as follows.

The universe is divided into three worlds: the elemental world of terrestrial nature; the celestial world of the stars; the supercelestial world of the spirits or intelligences or angels. Natural magic operates in the elemental world; celestial magic operates in the world of the stars; and there is a highest, religious, magic which operates in the supercelestial world. The lofty religious magus can conjure spirits or intelligences to his aid.[20] The enemies of this kind of magic called it diabolical conjuring, and indeed the pious believers in it were always aware of the danger of conjuring up evil spirits, or demons, instead of angels. Prospero has the conjuring power, and he performs his operations through the spirit, Ariel, whom he conjures. Of the two branches, Magia and Cabala, set out in Agrippa's handbook of Renaissance magic, Prospero would seem to use mainly the Cabalistic conjuring magic, rather than the healing magic of Cerimon, or the profound natural magic which pervades *The Winter's Tale*.

It is inevitable and unavoidable in thinking of Prospero to bring in the name of John Dee, the great mathematical magus of whom Shakespeare must have known, the teacher of Philip Sidney, and deeply in the confidence of Queen Elizabeth I. In his famous preface to Euclid of 1570, which became the Bible of the rising generations of Elizabethan scientists and mathematicians, Dee sets out, following Agrippa, the theory of the three worlds, emphasising, as does Agrippa, that through all the three worlds there runs, as the connecting link, number.[21] If I may paraphrase what I have myself said elsewhere, Dee was in his own right a brilliant mathematician, and he related his study of number to the three worlds of the Cabalists. In the lower elemental world, he studied number as technology and applied science. In the celestial world his study of number was related to astrology and alchemy. And in the supercelestial world, Dee believed that he had found the secret of conjuring spirits by numerical computations in the tradition of Trithemius and Agrippa.[22] Dee's type of science can be classified as 'Rosicrucian', using this word, as I have suggested that it can be used,[23] to designate a stage in the history of the magico-scientific tradition which is intermediate between the Renaissance and the seventeenth century.

The commanding figure of Prospero represents precisely that Rosicrucian stage. We see him as a conjuror in the play, but the knowledge of such a Dee-like figure would have included mathematics developing into science, and particularly the science of navigation in which Dee was proficient[24] and in which he instructed the great mariners of the Elizabethan age.

Now, if the first version of The Tempest appeared around 1611, the date at which Shakespeare chose to glorify a Dee-like magus is significant. For Dee had fallen into deep disfavour after his return from his mysterious continental mission in 1589, and he was completely cast off by James I after his accession. When the old Elizabethan magus appealed to James in 1604 for help in clearing his reputation from charges of conjuring devils, James would have nothing to do with him, in spite of his earnest protests that his art and science were good and virtuous and that he had no commerce with evil spirits.[25] The old man to whose scientific learning the Elizabethan age had been so deeply indebted was disgraced in the reign of James and died in great poverty in 1608.

Seen in the context of these events, Shakespeare's presentation of a scientific magus in an extremely favourable light takes on a new significance. Prospero is far from diabolic; on the contrary, he is the virtuous opponent of evil sorcery, the noble and benevolent ruler who uses his magico-scientific knowledge for good ends. Prospero might be a vindication of Dee, a reply to the censure of James. And the contemporary scientists and mathematicians who were working in the Dee tradition were to be found, not in the circle of the King, but in that of his son, Prince Henry. The Prince was eager to build up a navy, as Dee used to advise Elizabeth to do, and he patronised and encouraged scientific experts like William Petty who built for him his great ship, the *Royal Prince*. Mathematicians and navigators of the Elizabethan age, Walter Raleigh and his friend Thomas Hariot, were imprisoned by James in the Tower, but were encouraged by Prince Henry. Thus here the line of inquiry which seeks to establish that Shakespeare's Last Plays belong in the atmosphere and aspirations surrounding the younger royal generation makes contact with this other line of inquiry into the magico-philosophical influences in the plays. Prospero, the magus as scientist, would belong with Prince Henry and his interests, and not with those of his unscientific father with his superstitious dread of magic.

Thus I am suggesting new contexts in which to see *The Tempest*. This play is not an isolated phenomenon but one of the Last Plays, and other Last Plays breathe the atmosphere of learned magic, the medical magic of Cerimon in *Pericles*, the deep Hermetic magic of *The Winter's Tale*, the incantatory singing of *Henry VIII*. All such magics connect with one another and belong to the late period of Renaissance magic. *The Tempest* would be one of the supreme expressions of that vitally important phase in the history of the European mind, the phase which borders on, and presages, the so-called scientific revolution of the seventeenth century. Prospero is so clearly the magus as scientist, able to operate scientifically within his world view, which includes areas of operation not recognised by science proper.

There is also, and this is very important, the element of moral reform in Prospero's outlook and aims, the element of Utopia, an essential feature of the scientific outlook of the Rosicrucian period, in which it was seen to be necessary to situate the developing magico-scientific knowledge within a reformed society,[26] a society broadened by new moral insights to accept the broadening stream of knowledge. Prospero as scientist is also Prospero the moral reformer, bent on freeing the world of his island from evil influences.

Finally, we should see *The Tempest* in the context of *Henry VIII*, in which the reforming conciliatory themes of the Last Plays are presented through real historical personages. Henry VIII is seen as the monarch of the Tudor imperial reform, casting out vices in the person of Wolsey, and presenting a Reformation, originally Protestant, but in which the old hardness and intolerance has been done away in an atmosphere of love and reconciliation.

From these various lines of approach, *The Tempest* would now appear as the corner-stone of the total edifice of the Last Plays, the play presenting a philosophy which connects with all their themes and reflects a movement, or a phase, which can now be more or less identified among the currents of European intellectual and religious history. It is the Rosicrucian movement, which was to be given open expression in the manifestos published in Germany in 1614 and 1615.

In my book, *The Rosicrucian Enlightenment*, I have argued that this movement was connected with the currents stirring around the Elector Palatine and his wife. These were ostensibly Protestant, as befitted the head of the Union of German Protestant Princes, but drew on Paracelsist alchemy and other Hermetic influences for spiritual nourishment. The manifestos envisage a general moral and religious reform of the whole world. These strange hopes were to be extinguished in utter disaster, with the brief reign in Prague in 1619–20 of the 'Winter King and Queen' and the subsequent total defeat and exile of the unfortunate pair. Thus ended in ignominy and confusion the movement which had been building up around them in London, a movement very much weakened by the death of Prince Henry. Not only their own party in England but many in Europe had fixed their hopes on these two. And it would be wrong to say that all came to an end with the disaster, for the movement lived on, taking other forms, and leading eventually to important developments.

Shakespeare has often been derided for his absurd geographical error in giving a 'sea coast' to Bohemia in *The Winter's Tale*, but may his object have been to provide a setting for the frightful storm in which the infant Princess arrives in Bohemia? Shakespeare took the name 'Bohemia' from Greene's novel, *Pandosto*, the plot of which he was adapting.[27] Yet there is something strangely prophetic in his choice of a story about Bohemia, foreshadowing the terrible tempest of the Thirty Years' War which would break out in Bohemia following the shipwreck of the Winter King and Queen. Is it possible that Shakespeare may have known more of what was going on in Bohemia than do critics of his geographical ignorance? Might he, for example, have had some contact with Michael Maier, Paracelsist doctor and Rosicrucian, who was moving between Prague and London in the early years of the century, linking movements in England with movements in Germany and Bohemia?[28]

A main feature of the 'new approach' to Shakespeare's Last Plays presented here has been the argument that the hopes of a younger generation which the plays seem to express may allude to hopes in relation to a real historical generation, Prince Henry, and, after his death, Princess Elizabeth and her husband. Taken at its face value, this argument would amount to yet another 'topical allusion' detected in the plays, a type of investigation which has been very much used and abused. Even if the topical allusion to the younger royal generation is fairly substantially based, what does it amount to in relation to Shakespeare's genius, to the understanding of his mind and art? Topical-allusion hunting for its own sake is but an empty sport unless it can open doors to new approaches to matters more profound.

And it is precisely this, or so I believe, that this topical allusion can do. The other new approach attempted has been to the thought of the Last Plays, to the philosophy of nature with religious and reforming undercurrents, with association with scientific movements of the kind propagated by John Dee, with spiritual and mental enlightenment. And it is just such a movement as this which seems to have been associated in German circles with the Elector Palatine and with his disastrous Bohemian enterprise.

The German Rosicrucian movement was certainly not newly invented in connection with the Elector Palatine and his wife. It was something already in existence with which they, or the movement associated with them, became somehow involved. There are various influences from England on the movement which I have tried to bring out in my book, influences from Philip Sidney's mission to Germany and to the imperial court, influences from visits of the Knights of the Garter, influences from John Dee's sojourn in Bohemia. The second Rosicrucian manifesto of 1615 has included in it a discourse on secret philosophy which is based on Dee's *Monas hieroglyphica*.[29] The works of the Englishman, Robert Fludd, a leading exponent of Rosicrucian philosophy, were published at Oppenheim, a town in the territory of the Elector Palatine.[30] And, most curious of all from the theatrical point of view, there appears to have been an influence of English actors, or of plays acted by travelling English actors in Germany, on the ideas and modes of expression of the Rosicrucian publications.

The man known to be behind the movement, Johann Valentin Andreae, states in his autobiography that in his youth, around 1604, he wrote plays in imitation of English comedians,[31] and at about the same time he wrote the first version of his strange work, *The Chemical Wedding of Christian Rosencreutz*, first published, in

German, in 1616. This is a mystical romance reflecting cere-
monial of orders of chivalry in a setting which I believe I have
identified as the castle and gardens of the Elector Palatine at
Heidelberg,[32] reflecting his court there and the presence in it
of his English wife, the Princess Elizabeth. Andreae's style in all
his writings is dramatic, infused with theatrical influences. The
story of Christian Rosencreutz and his Order, told in the manifestos (which were not actually written by Andreae though
inspired by him),[33] is said to be a fiction or a play. And the
mysterious doings in the castle grounds in *The Chemical Wedding*
include a play, the plot of which is given as follows (I quote
from the résumé of it in my book):[34]

> On the sea-shore, an old king found an infant in a
> chest washed up by the waves: an accompanying letter
> explained that the King of the Moors had seized the
> child's country. In the following acts, The Moor
> appeared and captured the infant, now grown into a
> young woman. She was rescued by the old king's son and
> betrothed to him, but fell again into the Moor's power.
> She was finally rescued again but a very wicked priest
> had to be got out of the way. . . . When his power was
> broken the wedding could take place. Bride and
> bridegroom appeared in great splendour and all joined
> in a Song of Love:

> > This time full of love
> > Does our joy much approve. . . .

The plot reminds one of the plots of Last Plays, with shipwrecked
infants who grow up to have adventures in which evil influences
are surmounted, stories reflecting a passage of time from an
older generation to a younger, and ending in general love and
reconciliation. And, if I am right in my suggestions, this play
described in *The Chemical Wedding* is supposed to be enacted in
a setting reflecting the court of the Elector Palatine and the
Princess Elizabeth at Heidelberg. It is as though Shakespearean

dramatic influences in London at the time of their wedding were being reflected back to them through a mystical haze. The extremely simple plot of the comedy described in *The Chemical Wedding* is punctuated by Biblical allusions, as though the fiction had some reference to the religious problems of the day.

This is only one example of the curious reflections of plays, perhaps of plays staged by English players in Germany, in the German Rosicrucian literature. Was there some connection between players and Rosicrucian ideas? Ought we to look for light on Shakespeare in these directions? Did the Last Plays deliver a message the meaning of which we have lost? Are the connections between the Last Plays and the new generation of Prince Henry and his sister much more than topical allusions in the ordinary sense? Might they introduce us to ways of unravelling Shakespeare's position in the religious, intellectual, magical, political, theatrical movements of his time? Or, more than that, might they help us to penetrate to Shakespeare's inner religious experiences?

A French writer who has made a study of the Rosicrucian literature in relation to Shakespeare thinks that *The Chemical Wedding* reflects rituals of initiation through enaction of the mystery of death. He believes that some of Shakespeare's plays – he mentions particularly Imogen's death-like sleep and resurrection in *Cymbeline* – reflect such experiences, conveyed through esoteric allusion in the imagery.[35] He sees influences of 'spiritual alchemy' in the imagery of *Cymbeline*. The Rosicrucian method of using the play or the fiction as the vehicle through which to indicate an esoteric meaning would also be Shakespeare's method. I mention Arnold's book here not because I think it reliable as a whole, or in detail (it is not), but because the general drift of his comparative study of Rosicrucian literature and of Shakespeare may not be altogether wide of the mark.

Shakespeare died in 1616 and so did not live to hear the news of the events of 1620, the defeat at the Battle of the White Mountain, the flight of the Winter King and Queen of Bohemia, the outbreak of the Thirty Years' War. Perhaps that was the terrible storm which he prophetically dreaded.

It is strange that Shakespearean scholarship seems to have paid so much more attention to the biographical, the literary, or the critical aspects of its vast subject than to investigating Shakespeare's work in relation to the thought movements of his age. It is perhaps time that it should break out of the limits it has imposed on itself and begin to ask new questions. Even very familiar topics might appear in a new light if approached from new angles. I will give one example.

In 1623, Shakespeare's fellow-actors published that famous volume, the First Folio edition of his plays. *The Tempest* is the first play in the volume, which is dedicated to William Herbert, Earl of Pembroke, and his brother. We all know how this dedication has been worn threadbare by eager detectives pursuing clues to Shakespeare's personal history, but other questions might be asked about the First Folio. What was the attitude of its dedicatees to events and movements of the times? Pembroke and his brother had taken a conspicuous part in urging most strongly the support of the King and Queen of Bohemia in the great crisis of their lives, a support which was not forthcoming from James I. And one might also take into account the fact that, after their defeat and the collapse of their movement, violent propaganda was made against imaginary 'Rosicrucians' as diabolical 'conjurors'. The scare about Rosicrucians was in full swing in Paris in 1623,[36] the year in which Heminges and Condell fearlessly placed *The Tempest* in the forefront of their collection of Shakespeare's plays. I suggest that inquiries along these lines about the First Folio and its dedicatees might be rewarding, because they might be historically related to contemporary events and movements.

Let us now look back over the ground that has been traversed in these studies and attempt a summing up. Basically, their approach to Shakespeare has been historical, using history, not only in the literal sense of history of events, but in the sense of history of ideas as involved in history and expressed in imagery. The time chosen has been roughly restricted to the last years of Shakespeare's working life, and we have asked ourselves what were the historical events and situations which were of urgent importance in those years, and what was the imagery in which they were expressed. We have found that there was in those years a revival of Elizabethan traditions, centred on the younger royal generation, on Prince Henry and his sister. With this Elizabethan revival within the Jacobean age we have sought to connect Shakespeare's Last Plays, suggesting that in these plays he looks back to the inspirations of his youth and finds them, or hopes to find them, born anew in the younger generation. The working out of this suggestion involved, first of all, an examination of Prince Henry's ideas and circle and the discussion of what the Prince stood for in the wider field of European affairs and in the general European situation of Europe on the eve of the Thirty Years' War. We have found that Prince Henry held an important position in those years as a potential leader of European opposition to Spanish aggression. This was a stand rather different from that of his father, though it was presented in the same imagery, namely in a revival of the Tudor myth, now applied to the Stuarts, of the descent from the Trojan Brut and all that that involved in an accompanying panoply of revived Protestant chivalry of the age of Elizabeth. The interpretation of *Cymbeline* presented that play as a new formulation of Tudor British mythology, now applied to James and his children, and with enthusiastic approval of the Protestant wedding of Princess Elizabeth. *Cymbeline* therefore now comes out as the application of the Tudor mythology to the Stuarts by an old Elizabethan.

Such a revival included a return to the theology of John Foxe and his presentation of imperial reform, expressed in a modified and liberalised form in the Last Play of *Henry VIII*, and a return to the ideals of Philip Sidney, as romantically veiled in the *Arcadia*, which strongly influence *The Winter's Tale* and other Last Plays. And it involved a revival of respect for the Elizabethan type of magus, such as John Dee, and the presentation in

The Tempest of the traditions of Renaissance magic, now trans-
forming in the new age towards Rosicrucianism. The Elizabethan
revival when transported into Germany, would seem to coincide
with German Rosicrucianism, and it is one of the most fascinating
aspects of the Last Plays, as now interpreted, that they seem to
be anticipating in England, and before the departure of Princess
Elizabeth to Germany, modes of thought and feeling later to be
called Rosicrucian. Or were the two movements simultaneous?
That is to say, does the rising Rosicrucian movement in Germany,
the influence on which of Sidney, Dee and Bruno I have suggested
in my book, parallel and influence Shakespeare's development in
the Last Plays?

The new approach is thus really only a raising of new questions,
but they are questions which might eventually be answered
through the direction of Shakespearean research into new channels. We need intensive study of the neglected Prince Henry,
his circle, and all that he stood for. This would include pursuit
of the German contacts of Prince Henry, for example, Maurice,
Landgrave of Hesse. The Landgrave's intensely anglophile court
in the early years of the seventeenth century might surely show
traces, if not of Shakespeare himself, of a Shakespearean type of
approach to contemporary issues, and there is much unpublished
documentary material in Germany about the court of Maurice of
Hesse. It is possible that such researches might throw light on
what may have been the role of English actors in Germany.
Perhaps they were more than merely out-of-work actors seeking
to scrape abroad the living that they could not make at home.
Perhaps they were bearers and disseminators of the late Elizabethan Renaissance, and of Shakespearean ideas and ideals. The
major European figure who is closest to Shakespeare is Goethe,
and the Shakespearean influence on Goethe, and on the German
romantic movement generally, may ultimately derive from organic
connections developed in the earliest years of the seventeenth
century.

Thus the new approach to Shakespeare's Last Plays is a beginning, not an end. Nothing has been fully solved by these inquiries,

which raise new questions rather than answering old ones. They
are but indications of new paths which might be followed, new
ways which might be taken, by the Shakespearean scholars of the
future, which might – in course of time and after much future
labour – lead to a clearer understanding of where this towering
figure of William Shakespeare stands in the history of European
thought and religion.

Notes

1   *Bruno*, pp. 204 ff.
2   *Bruno*, pp. 356–7; *Astraea*, pp. 211–12.
3   *Pericles*, ed. F. D. Hoeniger, Arden edition paperback, 1969, Introduction,
    p. lxiii.
4   Ibid., pp. xv, lxxvi ff.
5   *Pericles*, III, ii, 31–2.
6   Ibid., pp. 95–6.
7   *RE*, pp. 44, 243, etc.
8   Ibid., p. 41.
9   *The Winter's Tale*, V, iii.
10 *Bruno*, pp. 35–40.
11 D. P. Walker, *Spiritual and Demonic Magic*, Warburg Institute, 1947
    (Kraus Reprint, 1967), pp. 164–70; *Bruno*, pp. 169 ff.
12 *Bruno*, pp. 211 ff.
13 These are the actual words of 'Hermes' in the *Asclepius*; see *Bruno*, pp. 39–
    40, 214–15.
14 *RE*, pp. 44, 245–8.
15 *The Tempest*, ed. F. Kermode, Arden edition paperback, 1954, Intro-
    duction, pp. xi ff.
16 Ibid., pp. xxi–xxiv.
17 *The Tempest*, IV, i, 13–34.
18 *Philaster*, I, ii, 195–205.
19 *The Tempest*, ed. F. Kermode, Introduction, p. xlviii.
20 *Bruno*, p. 131.
21 *Theatre*, p. 21.
22 *Bruno*, pp. 148–50; *RE*, p. xii.
23 'The Hermetic Tradition in Renaissance Science' in *Art, Science, and
    History in the Renaissance*, ed. Charles S. Singleton, Baltimore, 1968,
    p. 263; *RE*, pp. 220 ff.
24 *Theatre*, p. 29; Peter French, *John Dee*, Routledge & Kegan Paul, London,
    1972, pp. 171–2.

25 French, *Dee*, p. 10.

26 In one of the Rosicrucian manifestos, the movement is described as a 'General Reformation of the Whole Wide World'; see *RE*, pp. 42, 133 ff.

27 *The Winter's Tale*, ed. J. H. P. Pafford, Arden edition paperback, 1965, Introduction, pp. xxvii–xxxiii.

28 *RE*, pp. 81–2, 87–90.

29 *RE*, pp. 46–7. The influence of Dee on the German Rosicrucian movement is further attested by the appearance of his 'monas' sign in *The Chemical Wedding*, see *RE*, pp. 39, 61 and Pl. 19.

30 *RE*, Chapter VI, pp. 70 ff.

31 Ibid., p. 31.

32 Ibid., pp. 66–9.

33 Since publishing *RE*, I have come across a reference in the works of Leibniz stating that he (Leibniz) has been told that the Rosicrucian manifestos were written by Joachim Jungius (Leibniz, *Sämtliche Schriften und Briefe, Philosophische Schriften*, I, ed. P. Ritter, 1930, p. 275). This confirms the conjecture in *RE*, pp. 91–2.

34 *RE*, p. 63. A facsimile reprint of E. Foxcroft's English translation of the *Chymische Hochzeit* has now been published by John Warwick Montgomery, *Cross and Crucible*, The Hague, 1973, Vol. II. The passage about the plays is on pp. 408–10 (pp. 111–19 of the facsimile). Montgomery's determination to prove that Andreae was an 'orthodox Lutheran' somewhat mars his volumes for the historian of ideas.

35 Paul Arnold, *Esotérisme de Shakespeare*, Paris, 1955, pp. 177–200.

36 *RE*, pp. 103 ff.

5

A Sequel: Ben Jonson and the Last Plays

The Northcliffe Lectures ended where the last chapter ends, and the four chapters which form this book repeat, though with some revision, the text of the lectures. Rather than tamper with them by attempting new insertions, I have chosen to add to them this sequel. A separate study on 'Ben Jonson and the Last Plays' would have to repeat as an introduction the four preceding chapters. It has therefore seemed right to add to them the following study, though it must be emphasised that here also I present an 'approach' rather than a finished product.

It is rather curious that two remarkable plays treating of a similar subject from entirely opposite points of view should have appeared at about the same time, Shakespeare's *The Tempest* and Ben Jonson's *The Alchemist*. The central characters in these plays, Prospero and Subtle, are both concerned with occult sciences. In the one case the student of such sciences is presented as a noble magus, a religious reformer. In the other case he is presented as a charlatan and a cheat. The harsh realism of Jonson's satire is infinitely remote from the poetic vision of *The Tempest*, yet the student of the Last Plays should not neglect *The Alchemist*.

If only because of its date, *The Alchemist* demands attention. This play was first performed by the King's Men, Shakespeare's company, in 1610. It was first printed in 1612,[1] the year of Prince Henry's death, of the arrival of the Elector Palatine, of his betrothal to the Princess Elizabeth. This dating belongs exactly in the date complex of the Last Plays.

Ben Jonson has already appeared in this book for it was he who wrote the words for Prince Henry's masques, the 'Barriers' (1610), and 'Oberon' (1611), the charters (one might almost say) of the Elizabethan revival, echoed in *Cymbeline*. Why did not this established masque-writer produce a masque for Princess Elizabeth's wedding? A masque by Jonson for that wedding should have repeated, in yet more glorious forms, the themes of Prince Henry's masques in triumphs for his sister's wedding. But Jonson did not write a masque for that wedding; there is no record of one. In the following discussion of *The Alchemist*[2] it will appear that the theme of that play explains the omission.

Lovewit, the owner of a house in London, is away in the country because he is afraid of the plague, leaving a caretaker, Face, to look after the house. The caretaker falls in with Subtle, a rogue who uses his pretended skill in alchemy to cheat people out of their money. With the connivance of Face, he sets up alchemical paraphernalia in the empty house, and the two, aided by a doubtful female associate, Doll Common, are running a profitable business. Their dupes call at the house and the humour of the play consists in watching the various stratagems through which the skilful rogues cheat believers in alchemy. Their nefarious proceedings are shown up when Lovewit returns, unexpectedly early, to his house.

Jonson's extremely clever play is, first and foremost, a satire on alchemy as a deceptive science. With his usual industry, he had gone into the subject very thoroughly and the play shows much knowledge of alchemical procedure and terminology. Yet the satire covers far more than alchemical claims to make gold. It is not concerned with alchemy as an outmoded, medieval, gold-making illusion, but with alchemy in the modern, the contemporary sense, the sense in which Dee understood it. It satirises mathematics and mathematical magic; it satirises conjuring of spirits; it satirises Paracelsan medicine. In short, it is a satire on Rosicrucianism. The play is so rich in its knowledge of this movement, and so complex in its attack on it, that one cannot do more here than draw out a few threads.

Sir Epicure Mammon, full of greedy avarice, comes to the alchemist, intending to use the gold he is promised on vulgar self-indulgence. Mingled with his coarseness, Mammon shows mythological learning. He knows that the truths of alchemy are hidden in the fables of the poets, Jason's fleece, the Garden of the Hesperides[3]

> thousands more,
> All abstract riddles of our stone.

The alchemical interpretation of myth was worked out in great detail by Michael Maier, the contemporary German Rosicrucian. Maier's *Arcana arcanissima*[4] was not published until 1614, two years later than the printed edition of this play, but he was probably in touch with England earlier (we have suggested that he might have influenced Shakespeare).

Mammon's friend, Surly, doubts Subtle's wonderful experiments and ridicules his abstruse terminology. Subtle is ready with the argument that the alchemical terms hide deep truths, like other mystic forms of communication:[5]

> Was not all the knowledge
> Of the Egyptians writ in mystic symbols?
> Speak not the Scriptures oft in parables?
> Are not the choicest fables of the poets,
> That were the fountains, and first springs of wisdom,
> Wrapped in perplexed allegories?

At this exalted moment, when Subtle is expounding the lore dear to the religious alchemist which linked his 'work' with ancient truth concealed in myth and with Scriptural truth concealed in parables, Doll Common is perceived in the distance, and Surly, the doubter, delightedly exclaims that this explains all. Subtle's set-up is a bawdy house. Mammon is shocked. The alchemist, he maintains, is scrupulously virtuous, even to a fault, and is wronged by such suspicions.[6]

> No, he's a rare physician, do him right.
> An excellent Paracelsian. And has done
> Strange cures with mineral physic. He deals all
> With spirits, he. He will not hear a word
> Of Galen, or his tedious recipes.

This proves that Subtle is no old-fashioned medieval character, but very modern. He is a Paracelsist physician, using the new Paracelsist mineral medicines, and despising Galen. He is also a conjuror, dealing 'all with spirits'.

Other visitors to Subtle in search of alchemical gold are Ananias and Tribulation, holy brethren of Amsterdam. Their motive is not the vulgar one of Mammon, but the pious one of furthering their sect with the gold. Ananias is a little doubtful. The Brethren he represents have already advanced a good deal of money to Subtle for materials, and they have now heard that the work can be done more cheaply at Heidelberg:[7]

> they have heard since,
> That one, at Heidelberg, made it, of an egg
> And a small paper of pin-dust. . . .

Subtle persuades them to deal with him and expatiates on what the Stone can do for their cause. The gold it will make can be used to pay an army in the field, to buy out the King of France or the King of Spain. And through its medicinal use, they can make friends for the cause. Suppose they cure 'a lord that is a leper' with it, or illnesses of some knight or squire.[8]

One is very curiously reminded here of the first German Rosicrucian manifesto, the *Fama*, published in 1614 but in circulation before that date, which describes how one of the Rosicrucian Brothers is much spoken of in England because he 'cured a young earl of Norfolk of the leprosy'.[9] Since, as we shall see later, Jonson certainly had a good deal of knowledge of Rosicrucian literature, it is probable that he is indeed here referring to the *Fama*, which is said to have been circulated in 'four or five languages'.[10] Perhaps one of these manuscript versions was in English, and perhaps it was already circulating in England.

With Abel Drugger, we meet another class of dupe. Drugger is not a greedy knight, nor a fanatical Puritan. He is a tradesman, a tobacconist and druggist, who comes to consult Doctor Subtle (it is emphasised throughout that Subtle is a doctor) about a sign for his shop. Subtle proposes a design which will have magical power to 'strike the sense of the passers-by' and draw them into the shop:[11]

> He shall first have a bell, that's Abel;
> And by it, standing one whose name is Dee,
> In a rug gown; there's D and Rug, that's Drug;
> And, right against him, a dog snarling Er;
> There's Drugger, Abel Drugger. That's his sign.
> And here's now mystery and hieroglyphic.

As an Italian scholar has pointed out, this mnemonic image for Abel Drugger's name, which is also a mystical, magical hiero-glyph presenting the image of 'one whose name is Dee' is un-doubtedly a mocking allusion to Dee's famous work, the *Monas hieroglyphica*.[12]

Dee's mysterious 'monas', a hieroglyphic symbol composed of astral images, was believed by him to contain his whole philosophy. It was an alchemical sign, referring to alchemical secrets; it was Cabalistic, including angel-summoning secrets; it was mathematical, including the mathematical side of Dee's science. This unified, mystical-mnemonic sign encompassed in a unified hieroglyphic statement all Dee's exoteric magico-scientific activity, and his inner esoteric experience as an initiate into higher mysteries. It was, in fact, the Stone, the Philosopher's Stone, the initiation into reality reached by the adept, the wisdom which made possible his operational powers but which was in itself more important than those powers. At least, it was in some such way as this that Dee himself, and those who believed in him, regarded his 'monas' sign.[13]

Before coming to Subtle for advice about the sign for his

new shop, Drugger had already consulted him about the plan
of it. He shows the Doctor the plan. 'Here's the plot on't.'[14]

> And I would know, by art, sir, of your worship,
> Which way I should make my door, by necromancy,
> And where my shelves. . . .

Subtle gives the required advice:[15]

> Make me your door, then, south; your broad side, west:
> And on the east side of your shop, aloft,
> Write *Mathlai, Tarmiel, Valel, Thiel*,
> They are the names of Mercurial spirits. . . .

This satire again points unerringly to Dee, whose famous mathematical preface to the English translation of Euclid (1570)
grouped the mathematical arts in accordance with the definitions
of Vitruvius.[16] He was therefore an architectural expert, satiric-
ally shown as such by Jonson, in Subtle giving advice to a tradesman about the building of his shop. Dee's preface to the Euclid
was based on Agrippa on the three worlds. It was magical and
esoteric, but it was also exoteric and practical, intended to
give advice on the mathematical arts to artisans to help them in
their businesses and trades.[17] Abel Drugger, the tradesman, con-
sulting Doctor Subtle about the geomantic[18] design of his shop,
is obviously a clever hit at the mathematical preface of Doctor
Dee, the allusion being made quite obvious by the shop sign,
showing the image of 'one whose name is Dee'.

Whilst Dee is thus unmistakably present in the satire of Abel
Drugger, *The Alchemist* as a whole can now be seen as mainly
concerned with him, covering all the aspects of the 'monas',
alchemy, 'conjuring', mathematics and natural philosophy. The
philosophical and mathematical interests of Doll Common, the
Whore, point in his direction. She is very learned, and can
discourse of state secrets[19]

> Of mathematics, bawdry, anything.

Dee's activities with Kelley abroad[20] are hinted at, and are approved by the Whore. When Mammon is telling of Subtle's skill for which he has been courted by the Emperor 'above Kelley', Doll joins in with the enthusiastic remark:[21]

> Truth, I am taken, sir,
> Whole, with these studies, that contemplate nature.

Spoken by the Whore, this has a *double entendre*, and the identity of this philosophical Whore becomes a matter of some moment for the full understanding of the drift of the play.

For light on the Whore, we must turn to the dupe, Dapper. Poor Dapper is a clerk, who consorts with the small poets of the time and wants to have a familiar spirit to help him to win games. He is called a 'mere fool' by the knaves who fool him most cruelly. They tell him that he is much loved by 'the Queen of the Fairies'.[22] This excites him and he longs to see 'her royal Grace' who is 'a lone woman and very rich'.[23] He is rewarded by a vision of the 'priest of Fairy' and the Fairy Queen herself in her royal robes. The priest is Subtle in disguise; the Fairy Queen is impersonated by Doll Common. The unfortunate Dapper is blindfolded, robbed of everything he possesses by spurious elves and fairies, and imprisoned in the privy.[24]

What is Ben Jonson trying to do in these scenes? Surely, her royal Grace, the Fairy Queen, had an illustrious original. Was she not the heroine of Spenser's romance of Protestant chivalry glorifying Queen Elizabeth I, her chastity, justice, and other virtues? By fouling the sacred image of the Fairy Queen he would seem to be attempting to break the Elizabeth cult, associating it with his satire on what is basically the John Dee tradition. The destruction of the image of John Dee as the scientific life and soul of the Elizabethan age involves also the destruction of the image of the Queen he served.

The unbelieving Surly eventually exposes the gang by coming to consult them disguised as a Spanish Don, wearing a Spanish suit and speaking Spanish. Believing that he does not understand English they reveal their nefarious plans and practices.[25]

That the plot is exposed by a man in Spanish clothing enforces the already obvious political and religious application of this play. The Puritan immediately recognises the religious significance of Surly's Spanish clothes:[26]

They are profane
Lewd, superstitious, and idolatrous breeches.

The religious propaganda of that age was very easily reversed by using the same image with opposite intentions. Protestant Truth against Catholic error was turned round into Catholic Truth against Protestant error by opposite uses of the image of 'Truth the Daughter of Time'.[27] Similarly, the image of the Whore, representing an impure religion, could be used of either Protestant or Catholic error, according to the point of view.[28] The Fairy Queen against the Whore of Babylon had been the theme of Dekker's play, *The Whore of Babylon*, presented by Prince Henry's company of actors in 1607.[29] Thus Jonson, in this play which is obviously in the Spanish-Catholic interest, would have been at once understood in his presentation of the Fairy Queen as a Whore, as a false religion, accompanied by magic, alchemy, and other ideas and practices associated with John Dee.

What was Ben Jonson's object in presenting this elaborate politico-religious satire at this time? In 1610, when this play was acted, the match of Princess Elizabeth with the Elector Palatine was already rumoured; in 1612, when the Elector came to London to marry her, this play was printed. It would seem that Ben Jonson was not against Spanish matches but against Protestant matches, and in particular against the match with the Elector Palatine. It is significant that the Puritan mentions Heidelberg as a place where the successful making of the Stone is rumoured. Perhaps he knows that 'Rosicrucianism', stemming ultimately from John Dee's movement, has spread to Germany. The coming and going of emissaries between Germany and London during the years of preparation for the wedding was no doubt known to the omniscient Jonson, and, though the word 'Rosicrucian' is not mentioned in *The Alchemist*, it will be shown presently by quotation from other works by him, that Jonson knew a good deal about German Rosicrucian literature.

Thus it can now be explained, as promised, why Ben Jonson did not write a masque for Princess Elizabeth's wedding. He disapproved of it, like the Spanish ambassador who refused to attend. And he must have disapproved of the whole movement of Elizabethan revival around Prince Henry and Princess Elizabeth. Yet he had himself written Prince Henry's masques, so eloquent of that revival, and using the Elizabethan fairy imagery to decorate the Stuart use of the Tudor legend in the masque of 'Oberon'.[30]

How extremely strange it seems that in the year 1612, the year in which The Tempest was acted before Elizabeth and the Palatine, Shakespeare's friend, Ben Jonson, should have published a play satirising everything that The Tempest stands for, and which had been acted by Shakespeare's own company of players! Let us now turn to what really matters in all this discussion, the comparison between The Alchemist and The Tempest which is now possible.

The Italian scholar, Furio Jesi, already mentioned as having drawn attention to the satire on Dee's Monas hieroglyphica in the sign for Drugger's shop, has made an attempt at this comparison,[31] starting from the reflections of Dee in both plays. He notes that Prospero, like Dee, had a library and was a bibliophile, and that, like Dee, he produced a theatrical performance using mechanical contrivances, the masque in The Tempest being compared with Dee's production of a performance at Trinity College, Cambridge, involving use of a flying machine on account of which he was accused of magic.[32] Prospero, like Dee, was a magus, and it is Jesi's main point of contrast with The Alchemist that Shakespeare shows a good, not a demonic, magus, whereas Jonson shows neither a good nor a demonic magus, but a charlatan. Jesi thinks that Subtle's assistant, Face, reflects Kelley, and he emphasises that The Alchemist is opposed to the culture out of which The Tempest arises. Jesi makes an understanding approach to the difficult *Monas hieroglyphica*, which he thinks reflects an aristocratic and exclusive type of esotericism. He does not know Dee's preface to Euclid, and his exoteric activities as a teacher of artisans. Thus, although he identifies Dee in Drugger's shop sign, he misses the allusion here to Dee's mathematical preface which absolutely clinches the main object of Jonson's satire as undoubtedly Dee.

The understanding of both *The Alchemist* and *The Tempest* can now be carried much further by relating both plays to a contemporary situation in which Shakespeare is on one side, Jonson on an opposite side. To define the opposition as Protestant versus Catholic would be a misleading and much too narrow interpretation. On the one hand there is a 'Rosicrucian' type of culture, inheriting the traditions of Renaissance magic as expanded by alchemical and Paracelsist influence, an esoteric approach to religion involving tolerant and kindly attitudes to religious differences, and a hope of reconciliation through the younger generation. This is Shakespeare in *The Tempest* and in the Last Plays generally. On the other hand, there is a dislike and contempt for all such influences. This is Jonson in *The Alchemist*.

Or, if one thinks of the attitudes in both plays to the type of 'occult philosophy' taught by Agrippa, Shakespeare in *The Tempest* makes a positive use of this, to deepen and expand religious consciousness through a magical approach reaching into what is vaguely called the esoteric sphere. For Jonson, this is anathema, and all 'occult philosophy' is a cheat and a delusion.

Agrippa himself had oscillated in his attitudes. On the one hand he wrote the textbook of Renaissance magic, the *De occulta philosophia*; on the other hand he wrote a book arguing that all the sciences are vain, including the occult sciences.[33] Can one view *The Tempest* and *The Alchemist* as reflecting these two sides of Agrippa? No, for although Jonson may have used the *De vanitate* as a source, Agrippa's work is, at bottom, mystical, concerned with a 'learned ignorance', like that described by Nicholas of Cusa, in which the realisation of the vanity of all man's learning is in itself a mystical experience. There is nothing whatever of this in Jonson who shows only contemptuous dismissal in his attitude to the esoteric.

Jonson's mode of attack is through very clever ridicule. His play is extremely witty and would effectively dissolve all occult nonsense in mirth for many onlookers. But he achieves this success through coarse misrepresentation of the religious aims of pious alchemists, and through total lack of understanding of science, for example of Dee's mathematical science. Jonson is not only against occult science; he is against science itself. Or rather, all science, including mathematics, is for him occult, and therefore ridiculous.

What seems enlightened in Jonson's attitude is that he does not accuse Subtle of diabolism. He is not represented as in touch with evil and diabolical spirits but simply as a fraud. This apparently rational satire may seem to contrast favourably with the ferocious witch-scares to develop later among opponents of Rosicrucianism who accuse the adepts of diabolism. Yet Jonson's satire is extremely harsh and cruel, and is sadly prophetic of what will happen later in Germany when, after the defeat of the Winter King of Bohemia, Rosicrucianism and its literature will be stamped out with the utmost ferocity and savagely caricatured.

The reason why the comparison of *The Alchemist* with *The Tempest* is so important is because this establishes what before could only be conjectured, that Shakespeare is consciously defending Dee and his reputation. He is not only concerned with a nostalgic looking back to the Elizabethan age and its great magus, but is actively involved in a controversy in the present in which Dee is attacked. If *The Alchemist* was first acted in 1610 and *The Tempest* in 1611 their genesis was almost contemporaneous. If *The Tempest* was one year later than Jonson's play, it would seem like a reply to him. Or was Jonson replying to a version of *The Tempest* earlier than 1610 of which we have no knowledge? At any rate, and however this dating problem is to be solved, we are now aware of the startling revelation of an adverse attitude to *The Tempest* from within Shakespeare's own company of players. Shakespeare paints a portrait of Dee which is the very opposite of the contemporary portrait of him by Jonson. Shakespeare shows us an infinitely wise and beneficent figure, working for moral goodness and reform, a marvellous evocation of the Renaissance magus in his full imaginative and creative power. Jonson shows us a ridiculous quack, involved in a disreputable plot. These two portraits should hang side by side to be examined alternately by those interested in this controversial figure. The Jonson type of portrait held sway until quite recent years, during which much more has become known about John Dee's science and about the important place which he holds in the history of the Hermetic tradition at the points at which it is about to be transformed into the movements of the seventeenth century.[34]

And we now know more about Dee's influence on the German Rosicrucian movement[35] and about the connection of this with the movements around the Elector Palatine and his wife. Shakespeare's favourable attitude to their wedding, as compared with that of Jonson, forms an essential part of the problem.

To that wedding one constantly returns because it is a fixed historical point, the politico-religious meaning of which one can grasp. Those who approved of the wedding were those who were delighted by the Elizabethan revival and particularly by the revival of support for the Protestant cause abroad which it seemed to promise. Those who disapproved of it were the Spanish-Catholic party which feared it and tried to discredit and prevent it. Ben Jonson's *Alchemist* looks suspiciously like such an attempt. Nor may Jonson's line have been altogether displeasing to King James, even at the time of his daughter's betrothal. Though he allowed his daughter to marry the Elector Palatine, and spent so much money on her wedding, his purpose of encouraging a Spanish match for other members of his family really ran counter to the hopes raised by the Protestant wedding, as Prince Henry understood it, and as did many others both at home and abroad. After the death of Henry (one wonders what the Prince had thought of *The Alchemist*) James tended more and

more towards his policy of appeasement of Spain and it is therefore not surprising that Ben Jonson's attitudes suited him better
than Shakespeare's.

For Jonson continued to write the masques produced at
court before the King, and continued to introduce into them
satire in a similar vein to that which he had employed in
The Alchemist.

I have elsewhere pointed out[36] that Jonson's attacks in his later
masques on mathematicians, mechanics, joiners, 'mathematical
boys', though aimed primarily at Inigo Jones, reached back
through him to Dee's mathematical preface to Euclid and its
exposition of the mathematical arts. Inigo Jones was in the Dee
tradition, and this may well have been the root of the antagonism
between him and Jonson. Robert Fludd, disciple of Dee, is also
aimed at by Jonson.[37] The works of Fludd were published in the
Palatinate,[38] and so belong to the German, as well as the
English, Rosicrucian movement. Jonson's satire on mathematicians, alchemists, 'Rosicrucians', in the masques connects
in its general themes with the satire of *The Alchemist*, but I here
confine myself to only one of the 'Rosicrucian' passages in the
Jonsonian masques.[39]

In 1624, the masque of 'The Fortunate Isles and their Union',
on the familiar theme of 'Great Britain', opened with the entry
of Johphiel, described as 'an airy spirit and (according to the
Magi) the intelligence of Jupiter's sphere'. To this airy spirit
comes a melancholy student, one Mr Merefool, who is seeking
for the Rosicrucians but has found nothing. He is beginning to
wonder whether the Brotherhood really exists. Jonson had
evidently heard of the disappointing experiences of seekers after
Rosicrucians during the Rosicrucian furore in Germany. He had
certainly seen German Rosicrucian publications, for he describes
the engraving in Theophilus Schweighardt's *Speculum Rhodo-
stauroticum* of 1618 (reproduced as the frontispiece in my
Rosicrucian Enlightenment):[40]

> The castle in the air where all the brethren
> Rhodostaurotic live. It flies with wings
> And runs on wheels, where Julian de Campis
> Holds out the brandished blade.

Jonson is looking at the engraving, seeing the winged castle on wheels, the invisible college of the Rhodostaurotic (Rosicrucian) fraternity. Merefool is assured that he will be able to read at one view all books, speak all languages, and open all treasures; this is an echo of the promises in the Rosicrucian manifestos. When he asks how this is to be achieved, the answer is[41]

> Why, by his skill
> Of which he has left you an inheritance
> Here in a pot: this little gallipot
> Of tincture, high rose tincture. There's your order;
>
> > (*He gives him a rose.*)
>
> You will ha' your collar sent you ere't be long.

Merefool is being invested with an order, the emblem of which is a rose, founded by one who has left an alchemical inheritance. This must be Christian Rosencreutz, and Jonson is perhaps here satirising the mystical initiation ceremonies in *The Chemical Wedding*.

Merefool longs to be 'tinctured' so that he may have visions. He longs particularly to see Zoroaster and Hermes Trismegistus but is told that they are too busy to appear. As a consolation he is shown a masque of old English poets which he much enjoys, and is sorry when the show vanishes; he wanted to show himself grateful for it since this is the first boon he has received from the Company of the Rosy Cross. To which Johphiel replies with infinite scorn[42]

> The company o' the Rosy Cross, you widgeon!
> The company of players! Go, you are
> And will be still yourself, a Merefool. . . .

In Ben Jonson's satire, Rosicrucians melt into players, or Rosicrucians are players, or the Rosicrucian legend and literature about which he has shown considerable knowledge, dissolve into theatre. Ask for Rosicrucians, and the only real people you will see will be stage-players, acting their parts.

These clever imitations of Rosicrucian mystifications are quite in keeping with Johann Valentin Andreae's insistence that the Rosicrucian myth is 'theatre' or a 'play-scene'. Presumably Jonson is taunting some person or persons unknown, showing that he knows their secrets. Does he know that actors, or some actors, are Rosicrucians, whatever that may mean? Does he know that Rosicrucian actors have been in contact with Rosicrucians in Germany? Is he hinting at a movement, spreading through actors and the stage, and linking England and Germany?

The date of this satire is significant, for by 1624 the Thirty Years' War was in full swing in the areas of Germany where Rosicrucianism had flourished, the German Rosicrucian literature was proscribed, and, as far as possible, destroyed, the King and Queen of Bohemia were in poverty-stricken exile at The Hague. Their movement had ended in disastrous failure, and with it had collapsed a hope of a liberal alternative to the Spanish-Hapsburg version of the Counter Reformation, now in control of nearly the whole of Europe.

Shakespeare, fortunately, did not live to see this. He had died in 1616 but he was not forgotten, for in 1623 his loyal friends among the King's Men had published the First Folio edition of his works, with *The Tempest* in the forefront. Allusion to *The Tempest* in a masque presented before King James in 1624 would therefore be quite topical. Is there not such an allusion in the name 'Johphiel' of Jonson's 'airy spirit'?[43] Surely this would remind the audience of Ariel, and the further inference would be that the creator of Ariel was connected with a Rosicrucian movement expressed through actors and the stage.

The attitude of Ben Jonson towards Shakespeare has always seemed uneasy, a mixture of somewhat patronising words of praise mingled with a good deal of criticism of an apparently literary character. Shakespeare wanted art, had small Latin and less Greek, was too copious, ought to have 'blotted' many of his lines, was old-fashioned, *Pericles* a mouldy old tale, and so on. It is rather curious to notice that Jonson's preface to the reader before *The Alchemist* contains literary criticism of this type; it speaks of 'those who utter all they can, however unfitly', for it is 'the disease of the unskilful to think rude things greater than unpolished'. This might be directed at someone who 'wanted art', yet the critical attack in *The Alchemist* is not about wanting art in the literary sense but about being connected with John Dee's alchemy, conjuring, mathematics, and plots with the Fairy Queen. Perhaps an undercurrent of very deep opposition to Shakespeare on politico-religious grounds ran below the surface of Jonson's attempts to get rid of his influence by superior references to his want of art.[44]

In following the line of Ben Jonson's antagonism to *The Tempest* we have reached the same point as that reached in the last Northcliffe Lecture, where it began to appear that the Last Plays are already formulating in England the movement associated with the Elector Palatine in Germany. Let us call this movement Rosicrucian, whatever that may mean. The analysis of Jonson's hostility to it has again suggested that Shakespeare was connected with it, and with its spread through the theatre. Moreover, the Rosicrucian manifesto – the *Fama* and its symbolism – seems known both to Jonson and to Shakespeare, used negatively by the one, positively by the other. The great Rosicrucian controversy had already broken out in London, before the wedding.

There is much that is still very obscure here but I have added this chapter, brief and inadequate though it is, as an indication that Jonson's opposition to the Last Plays belongs to the subject of this book. It is the dark side which throws into relief the Shakespearean themes of love and reconciliation. It was only within the magical world of the Renaissance that happy solutions based on love and magic could seem possible, and the Renaissance world was threatened.

Notes

1 E. K. Chambers, *The Elizabethan Stage*, London, 1923, III, p. 371.
2 Ben Jonson, *Works*, ed. C. H. Herford and Percy Simpson, Oxford University Press, 1937, V, pp. 286–407. Quotations are in modernised spelling, as in the edition in the New Mermaid series, edited by Douglas Brown, 1965.
3 II, i, 103–4.
4 *RE*, pp. 80–1. (The *Arcana arcanissima* was *not* dedicated to Sir William Paddy as I have there stated in error.)
5 II, iii, 201–7.
6 II, iii, 229–33.
7 II, v, 70–1. Cf. also the mention of Heidelberg at III, ii, 36.
8 III, ii, 20–41 ('the lord that is a leper', line 37).
9 The *Fama* states that the 'R.C. Brother' who cured the young earl of leprosy was the first of the Brotherhood to die, and that he died in England (*Fama*, quoted *RE*, p. 244). See also *RE*, p. 196 (quotation by Ashmole of the statement in the *Fama* about healing the leper).
10 *RE*, p. 250 (*Fama*); p. 254 (*Confessio*). Cf. also *RE*, p. 237.
11 II, vi, 19–24.
12 Furio Jesi, 'John Dee e il suo sapere', *Comunità*, no. 166, April 1972, p. 287.
13 C. H. Josten, 'A Translation of John Dee's *Monas hieroglyphica*', *Ambix*, XII (1964), pp. 155–65. Cf. *RE*, pp. xii, 38–9, 107–8, 197–8 etc. The 'monas' sign really represented the essence of 'Rosicrucian' alchemy, of which orthodox alchemists disapproved; it included 'conjuring' (cf. *Bruno*, pp. 148–50).
14 I, iii, 10–12.
15 I, iii, 63–7.
16 *Theatre*, pp. 20–40.
17 Ibid., pp. 40–1.
18 See Maurice Freedman, *Geomancy*, Presidential Address to the Royal Anthropological Institute, Proceedings, 1968, p. 5. Freedman quotes the plans for Drugger's shop in *The Alchemist* and compares these with the principles of Chinese geomancy.
   Since Drugger is a satirical portrait of Dee, his geomantic shop-plan can be interestingly compared with my suggestion that Dee might have been consulted about the plan of Burbage's Theatre (*Theatre*, pp. 107–11).
19 II, iii, 257.
20 On these see *RE*, pp. 37–40; R. J. W. Evans, *Rudolf II and his World*, Oxford University Press, 1973, pp. 218–28. Evans sees Dee's mission in Bohemia as a very serious advocacy of world reform, based on his mystical experiences.
21 IV, i, 95.
22 I, ii, 106.
23 I, ii, 155.

24 III, iv, v.
25 IV, iii.
26 IV, vii, 48–9.
27 F. Saxl, 'Veritas Filia Temporis', *Philosophy and History*, essays presented to E. Cassirer, Oxford University Press, 1936, pp. 197–222.
28 On Catholic use of the Whore image of Queen Elizabeth I, see *Astraea*, pp. 80–1; *Academies*, p. 225.
29 Thomas Dekker, *The Whore of Babylon, As it was acted by the Princes Servants*, London, 1607; modern edition, Dekker, *The Dramatic Works*, ed. Fredson Bowers, Cambridge University Press, 1955, II, pp. 491–588. The personage of Titania, the Fairy Queen, is said to figure 'our late Queen Elizabeth', whilst the Empress of Babylon figures Rome. The play opens with a dumb show on the theme of Truth, the daughter of Time, with Truth on the side of the Fairy Queen.
30 See above, p. 29.
31 In his article cited above (n. 12).
32 On this performance, see *Theatre*, pp. 3, 29–32.
33 Agrippa's *De occulta philosophia* was published in 1510; his *De incertitudine et vanitate scientiarum*, in which he seems to oppose the earlier book, appeared in 1526. On the two books and the problems they raise, see C. G. Nauert, *Agrippa and the Crisis of Renaissance Thought*, University of Illinois Press, 1965, pp. 201 ff., 175–7, 196 ff.; *Bruno*, pp. 130–43, 259–62.
34 *Theatre*, pp. 1–8; Peter French, *John Dee*, Routledge & Kegan Paul, London, pp. 4 ff.
35 *RE*, pp. 30–41, 45–7 etc.
36 *Theatre*, pp. 86–90.
37 Ibid., p. 90.
38 *RE*, pp. 70–102.
39 Ben Jonson, *Works*, ed. cit., VII, pp. 710–22. Quotations in modernised spelling are from Ben Jonson, *The Complete Masques*, ed. Stephen Orgel, Yale University Press, 1969, pp. 433–53.
40 *Masques*, ed. Orgel, pp. 435–6.
41 Ibid., p. 437.
42 Ibid., p. 446.
43 'Iohpiel' is mentioned as the name of a spirit connected with Jove or Jupiter in Henry Cornelius Agrippa's *De occulta philosophia*, ed. K. A. Nowotny, Graz, 1967, p. 160. The name 'Ariel' can also be found in Agrippa's work (p. 223), described as the name of an angel.
44 Thomas Fuller, speaking in 1662 of the 'wit combats' between Ben Jonson and Shakespeare, compares them to engagements between a 'Spanish great Gallion' and an 'English man of War' (quoted Chambers, *William Shakespeare*, London, 1930, II, p. 245).

Epilogue

The understanding of Shakespeare's Last Plays has suffered from the gap in our knowledge caused by the failure of the Elizabethan revival in England, due to its eventual discouragement in favour of the Spanish interest by James I, and the failure and suppression of the German extension of the movement in the Thirty Years' War. The strength of the enthusiasm in England for both movements has been curiously minimised by historians who tend to emphasise the wisdom of James in keeping his Great Britain out of the war. This may be a right historical and political judgment so far as Great Britain is concerned, but it leaves out of consideration Europe as a whole, anxiously looking for a leader in James against the threatening storm and finding, after the misleading promise of the wedding, only withdrawal and dissimulation, and even indirect sabotage of the cause of his daughter and her husband. To look at these situations from Shakespeare's point of view really demands a new approach to the history of those years, obviously too enormous a task for these brief afterthoughts.

We have arrived at Shakespeare by an unaccustomed route and we are now able to see him in an unaccustomed light, or rather, if we still do not see him, we begin dimly to grasp where he stands amid the currents and cross-currents of magic and religion, of Reformation and Counter Reformation, whipped up in these years towards the oncoming storm of the Thirty Years' War.

The important fact for the historical understanding of the Last Plays is the fact of the Elizabethan revival, and to understand that we need to understand the Elizabethan age and what it was that was being revived. It may be doubted whether the Elizabethan period is as yet understood as a thought-movement, or a movement of ideas, though other aspects of it have been so elaborately studied. What was the philosophy of the Elizabethan age? Who were its characteristic thinkers? How far were they influenced by Renaissance philosophy or Renaissance magic? Again, these are questions too vast for an epilogue, though one Elizabethan thinker has been touched on in this book, John Dee.

Dee was an uninhibited magus, who attempted to operate Agrippa's occult philosophy on all its three levels, and whose powerful influence on the Elizabethan age, on the Queen herself, on aristocracy and artisans, on the shaping of the Elizabethan imperial idea, has yet to be fully realised. Through his connection with Sidney and the Sidney tradition, through his own continental mission, Dee's influence percolated far and wide. Hence the Elizabethan revival included a Dee revival, and this coincided with the Dee revival in the German Rosicrucian movement.

Dare one say that this movement reaches a peak of poetic expression in *The Tempest*, a Rosicrucian manifesto infused with the spirit of Dee, and using (like Andreae) theatrical parables for esoteric communication?

In Catholic Europe, Renaissance influences were being severely discouraged in the Counter Reformation. The death of Giordano Bruno had initiated a strong movement of repression of Renaissance philosophy.[1] Works canonical in the Renaissance, such as Francesco Giorgi's *De harmonia mundi* (which infuses the Rosicrucian musical philosophy), fell under suspicion. The new Aristotelianism in both philosophy and literary criticism was a check on Renaissance Neoplatonism. This stemming of the Renaissance currents was taking place in Europe generally. In

France, the Neoplatonism of the French Renaissance, of which Baïf's Academy of Poetry and Music was an outstanding product, was giving way before the new tendencies.

In this difficult and novel task of trying to place Shakespeare in the Hermetic tradition it is important, at this stage, to avoid imposing too hasty definitions, though we may be beginning to see him as belonging to the late outburst of esoteric and magical thinking in a world in which such ideas are in danger. The opposition of Ben Jonson might, in one of its aspects, be defined as Counter Reformation influences being used, not only politically in a pro-Spanish direction, but also philosophically, to control and discourage Renaissance traditions.

Some Renaissance influences, on the religious side, seem to have survived in Freemasonry, which is somehow connected with Rosicrucianism,[2] though this is a difficult problem. It may be the answer to those liturgical experiences reflected in *The Chemical Wedding* and possibly hinted at on the esoteric levels of Shakespearean drama. Perhaps this is why *The Tempest* reminds us of *The Magic Flute*.

There are many old problems which might show up in a new light through the new approach, for example Shakespeare and Francis Bacon. This is one of the areas which have been rendered almost inaccessible to serious research through being occupied by pseudo-scholarship. Let me state clearly that I am absolutely convinced that the real author of the works of Shakespeare was Shakespeare. Yet there is probably a link between Bacon and Shakespeare for they belong in the same line of country. Bacon wrote a masque for Princess Elizabeth's wedding and was her friend; Bacon's *New Atlantis* is full of Rosicrucian influence.[3] Bacon and Shakespeare *are* close and it is important to compare and contrast them sensibly. I have suggested elsewhere that the reason for Bacon's curious underestimate of mathematics in his natural philosophy might have been because he was afraid of Dee's reputation.[4] We have seen how Jonson used Dee's mathematics in his attack. Such ferocity would have frightened Bacon, whose philosophy was so largely drawn from the Renaissance

EPILOGUE

Hermetic tradition and who had to placate James. We begin to understand that *The Tempest* was a very bold manifesto, and that Shakespeare was braver than Bacon.

The unease of the later years of the reign of James, when the Elizabethan revival is unacknowledged and half-suppressed, introduces a twist into the history of thought which it is hard to disentangle. The masque in *The Tempest*, with its emphasis on chastity, belongs to the Elizabethan revival, and is like a complex Elizabeth-portrait, now applied to Princess Elizabeth. The later Ben Jonson masques for James show a shift of emphasis, away from the tone of the Prince Henry masques, away from the discouraged Elizabethan revival, and towards the Jacobean absolutism. Jonson flatters James most fulsomely in these masques, as absolute monarch, an attitude more in keeping with Spanish-Hapsburg influence than with the liberal monarchy of Elizabethan tradition. Owing to this deflection of Elizabethan tradition into Jacobean absolutism, the Puritan trend in the Elizabethan tradition becomes lost to sight and is confused with the imagery of the Stuart monarchy. The Caroline absolutism was of a different tinge from the Jacobean, not pro-Spanish, an Anglicanism influenced by French revival of Platonism,[5] favourable to Shakespeare.[6] But it further discredited courtly chivalry in the eyes of the Puritans, and Milton gave up his plan of writing an Arthurian epic. Yet the Elizabethan tradition which, despite its courtly trappings, was Puritan in ethics, continued (Milton's *Comus* comes out of it), and made contact with Puritanism proper in the Revolution. To this continuity is, I believe, due the fact that Hermetic influence, and in particular the influence of Dee, is strong among Puritans of the Commonwealth period.[7] One can see in Jonson's *Alchemist* how the antagonism to Dee is associated with antagonism to Puritanism. And the unpublished papers of Isaac Newton have revealed that the great mathematician and Puritan was an enthusiastic student of the kind of literature which is derided in *The Alchemist*. Newton was deeply interested in the alchemical interpretation of myth and in the works of Michael Maier.[8]

Thus Shakespeare, and not Jonson, was in the line leading to the advance of science. There is much food for thought for the historian of ideas in the positive and negative presentations of Dee by Shakespeare and Jonson.

Elizabeth of Bohemia represented the principle of Protestant opposition to the Catholic powers, so dear to Puritans, and which, as our studies have shown, was strongly Hermetic in its Rosicrucian manifestations. After many vicissitudes, the principle of the Protestant Succession ensured the triumph of a Protestant form of monarchy for Great Britain, and George I ascended the British throne. He was, needless to say, the grandson of Elizabeth of Bohemia, and, through the Hanoverian line, Queen Victoria was likewise her descendant. Thus Princess Elizabeth did indeed become 'mother of nations', as prophesied in the 'Barriers', and ancestress of the Victorian British Empire. One of her biographers, who writes in the Victorian tradition, obviously has Victoria in mind when contemplating the staunch Protestantism of her heroine.

It is perhaps fanciful to end this study with an allusion to Tennyson's *Idylls of the King*. Yet, after immersing ourselves in the historical situation surrounding Elizabeth of Bohemia, the Victorian age looms as her very distant and transformed successor. Tennyson's *Idylls* celebrate the Victorian ethic of the gentleman in the form of a poem using the Arthurian legends, dedicated to the memory of Victoria's late German husband, an 'ideal knight', dear to science (Albert had organised the Crystal Palace Exhibition glorifying the marvels of modern science), far-sighted enemy of war,

> Voice in the rich dawn of an ampler day.

Far in the past, among the old, unhappy, far-off things and battles long ago, are now the agonies of that painful age of witch-hunting and religious wars, and with calm confidence the Victorian seer contemplates the advance of science, and celebrates the Monarch and Empress in terms of Arthurian romance. The Elizabethan chivalric Puritanism survives to become the vehicle of Victorian ethic, the millennial vision of an ampler day continues the Rosicrucian dream, the *Idylls of the King* are a distant successor to *Cymbeline*. For pious Victorians, the Bible and Shakespeare were the props of British character, nor could anyone doubt for a moment that Prospero's magic was good, the pleasing accompaniment of a romantic moral tale, harmless as Aladdin's Lamp in a pantomime for the children.

We who have seen the collapse of that dream, too, into even more frightful wars and terrible witch-hunting, can return to Shakespeare's Last Plays with a deeper sense of the knife-edge of danger on which they were poised. This book has endeavoured to provide new approaches to their meaning, through which we can begin to understand how Shakespeare in the last years of his life saw a vision of a wide imperial peace, in the religious sense, about to be realised. Its failure, and the failure of the young people on whom he fixed his hopes, emerge as a Shakespearean tragedy on a vast scale.

Notes

1 The most recent study of this repressive movement is that by A. Rotondo, 'La censura ecclesiastica e la cultura', in *Storia d'Italia*, V, Einaudi, Turin, 1973, pp. 1399–492.

2 *RE*, pp. 206–19.

3 Ibid., pp. 6, 118–27.

4 Ibid., pp. 123–5.

5 See *Astraea*, pp. 210–11.

6 Charles I enjoyed a performance of *Cymbeline*; see Chambers, *William Shakespeare*, London, 1930, II, p. 352.

7 John Webster, a Puritan divine in the Commonwealth period, enthusiastically admired Dee's preface to Euclid; see P. M. Rattansi, 'Paracelsus and the Puritan Revolution', *Ambix*, XI, pp. 19–20; *RE*, pp. 185–7.

8 See J. E. McGuire and P. M. Rattansi, 'Newton and the Pipes of Pan', *Notes and Records of the Royal Society*, 21 (1966), pp. 108–41; P. M. Rattansi, 'Newton's Alchemical Studies' in *Science, Medicine, and Society in the Renaissance*, ed. A. G. Debus, London, 1972, II, pp. 167–83; *RE*, pp. 205 ff.

Index